Cosmic Reiki

A Metaphysical Healing Journey
Learn how to love yourself
Let go and heal the Past

S'Roya Rose

3RD EYE
PUBLICATIONS

COSMIC REIKI

Copyright © S'Roya Rose, 1997
First Edition Printed 2000
Revised Edition 2012
Reprinted 2014

All rights reserved. No part of this publication, either in part or in whole, may be reproduced, transmitted or utilised in any form, by any means, digital, electronic, photographic, or mechanical, including photocopying, recording or by any information storage system, without permission in writing from the author, except for brief quotations embodied in literary articles and reviews, credit to be given to author S'Roya Rose.

ISBN 978 0 9923123 9 8

Also by the author:
In Search of Soul
The Art of Meaningful Living
The Elegance of Being
Embracing the Power of the Goddess
Modern Goddess Oracle
Blue Moon Oracle
S'Roya Rose TAROT

Acknowledgement

During the course of my life there have been many events, people, situations and places that have influenced its course. However, nothing could have prepared me for the giant leap in consciousness that I would experience which learning Reiki provided for me. I can only thank this energy that I cannot see with love and gratitude from the depths of my heart. For it has afforded me with amazing insights into my life and the things that unfolded as I healed my hearts wounds with ease, joy and love.

I would like to thank and honour Nada Watkins my first initiating master, my mother Shaman Eilee, who initiated me into my Masters, my 2nd husband Brian Priest (who originally helped me publish my first 2 books) and my two wonderful daughters, Tamaya and Cortnei, for their unwavering support of my spiritual growth with whom I shared this journey. I wish to thank all my students and all the Reiki Masters I met on this journey and who went before me for sharing their truth, love and enlightenment with me.

Blessings to you all.

My Dedication

This book is dedicated to those who bravely choose Cosmic Reiki as a Spiritual Pathway, leading them through complete self-transformation, inner healing and ultimately to wholeness.

CONTENTS

8	Introduction
13	My Story Begins

PART ONE

20	Why Reiki?
31	The Awakening
60	Becoming Energy Conscious

PART TWO

80	The Next Step
94	The Doors of Perception
111	A Rite of Passage
119	Doorway to the Divine

PART THREE

130	The Challenge of Mastership
147	Controversial Teachings
161	Gateway to the Cosmos
177	The Independent Reiki Association
185	21 Day Reiki Cleanse
188	Other Books & Oracles by the Aurthor

INTRODUCTION

During the course of my life there have been many events, people, situations and places that have influenced its course. However, nothing could have prepared me for the giant leap in consciousness that I would experience which learning Reiki would provide.

As one begins the sacred journey of looking for truth, love and enlightenment a huge awakening process begins. This awakening sparks unconscious feelings and ideas that urge the inner self to look for answers to many of life's questions. When a person is ready and wants to begin their spiritual journey something usually shows up to help light their pathway. Reiki shows up for many.

Reiki is a spiritual energy that touches one's own spiritual nature, gently encouraging it to move forward seeking the road back to wholeness. It awakens a sleeping spirit to the abundance and joys of the experience of life on all levels of mind, body, emotions and spirit.

Reiki teaches us by a process of transforming one's energies of mind, body, emotions and spirit from the lower negative energies (of ego) to the higher positive energies (of the soul), taking oneself from fear to love. During this process much of the past is left behind as one embraces the inner self or soul. It marks a time of deep cleansing and purification and by its very nature this takes each individual on a personal spiritual journey within.

My whole journey through Reiki has been one of self-realisation and inner healing and enlightenment and this is how I teach it and pass it onto others who wish to use it.

Here in the West it seems we have mainly focused on the metaphysical science/energy aspects or on the healing aspects of this vibrational energy and little if anything has been taught as a path of self-realisation through the realms of Reiki. This book hopes to deal with the spiritual journey aspects of this healing energy.

Over the years we have seen many changes in the way Reiki has been taught. Individual Masters have sought to tailor it to suit their understanding of their personal journey through the use of Reiki, and I respect that. As individuals we can only share with others what has happened to us and what we have gained as wisdom through those experiences and this can differ from Master to Master. Reiki Masters simply become masters of their own energies of mind, body, emotions and spirit and eventually wish to share this path with their students.

In some of the original Japanese teachings Reiki had as many as seven levels, which helped to illuminate one's mind through the path of self-healing before obtaining master's status. These were to be of assistance to students as they worked closely with their chosen master while treading the path of self-realisation and enlightenment. We, in the West, have long since abandoned such rigidity because our culture is more flexible. However, I feel that the three levels that are now taught are a middle path and are most acceptable as adequate stages of progression, full of comprehensive teachings.

The journey of self-realisation and enlightenment takes time and does not arrive with attunements in a weekend. It is through the regular application and practice of Reiki that helps to bring about self-awareness as it balances our energy field from negative to positive. Reiki gently transforms the lower body by allowing any negative beliefs, attitudes, behaviors, emotional responses or past traumas (that have long been forgotten by the conscious mind), to surface and be gently released. Once they are allowed to be released the higher self recognises this process and begins to urge us to let go of more things that are self-defeating. This process can take many years for some, as they need to heal the physical body as well as the mental/emotional aspects of themselves.

The West has become obsessed in its pursuit of health and has focussed mainly on the physical healing aspects of Reiki. However, unless we deal with all aspects of a person, full recovery from any illness, it is unlikely to last, as some form of reoccurrence can often occur. This new realisation has seen the rise of many metaphysical healing modalities that can assist with this process. Inner doubts and fears show up in our life in many ways but by the time it shows up in the physical body it is already chronic and needs immediate attention on all levels. The body is always the last messenger of the soul and we simply cannot ignore it.

Reiki has the effect of shedding light on a very special part of us that has been lying dormant or shut away from view. It has the sensations of a rebirth in consciousness, giving life a new meaning as we embrace these spiritual aspects. This then helps with our connection with the higher self or soul. It is this kind of deep spiritual development within a person over time that can see them leave behind the need to experience all kinds of depression, illness, aches and pains.

My experience is that the attunements of Reiki help reconnect the soul to the energy of the spirit and are profound to say the least. However, there is a need for guidance as the spirit remembers the soul's path as it navigates the deep healing that needs to take place on all levels.

So how does it work?

Imagine that you are at the beginning of an escalator (symbolic of your soul's spiritual healing path) but want to move along at your own pace and in your own time. So every time you wish to make a move forward you have to press a special button (symbolic of a Reiki self-treatment). As you treat yourself with Reiki energy it has the effect of gently moving you along your spiritual path. It does this by helping you to let go of the past, through acceptance and forgiveness while making the relevant shifts in consciousness that are required for your highest good at the time by your higher self. As this happens your awareness grows, allowing you a better experience of your life. During this whole process you remain in control as you have the button and press it at will. The more treatments you give yourself the faster you heal yourself as you transform your lower body with your higher nature. This is your soul's true destiny, and begins the quest for more knowledge about who it is, why it has come, and what is can contribute to the betterment of mankind.

As spiritual beings looking for our Holy Grail of inner truth, love and enlightenment, the journey is about coming to terms with oneself on all levels, finding wholeness of the spirit is the just the first part. There are many aspects of this journey that each individual faces and it helps to have some tools along the way. Reiki is just one tool that is multi-facetted and can be used to recharge the batteries and gather oneself up, no matter how old or where you are or what your situation is. It can be used to clear the mind and find clarity, helping discernment while enhancing well-being. It allows for self-love to enter the chambers of the heart, which seek to serve self and others with respect, love and honor. It invites the divine into our lives as we recognise our connectedness to all things, that we are, in fact, part of the whole universe, not separate from anything. It lets us know that there are only two energies in the universe – one is fear, the other is love – and that we have the choice in any given moment, which one we wish to project. I have always chosen LOVE.

My hope is that as you read this book you are inspired to begin or continue your spiritual journey with the use of this energy as one of your metaphysical tools.

Many Blessings on your pathway
S'RoyaRose
Independent Reiki Master/Teacher.

You can contact S'Roya via;
email@sroyarose.com
www.sroyarose.com

How My Reiki Story Began...

Before I discovered Reiki I considered myself to be an ordinary woman battling her way through life as a divorcee, mother of two daughters with a hairdressing business to run and a mortgage to pay. Like many before me, I had been through a myriad of life crises, finally wrestling them all to the ground in my early thirties. I felt strong and in charge of my life, having had a good dose of what I considered to be reality, at least I thought so. What I didn't know, was my life was about to under go a dramatic change yet again.

My mother, whom I hadn't seen for many years, came to live with me. Her marriage of 30 years to my father had finally ended and her health had begun to slide, eventually turning into what we now know to be severe chronic fatigue.

We went through the process of elimination through the usual gambit of medical analysis, which was the only way they could find out what was wrong with my mother, and give it a name. We discovered that medical science and doctors could do very little or nothing to help my mother and her illness.

During this time we learnt a great deal about each other as women and a deep respect and bond grew between us as we shared our thoughts and feelings about men, love, business, family and marriage. I felt that for the first time in my life that my mother and I had become best friends and I know she felt the same. It was a very special time filled with love and frustration, as I wanted nothing more than to help my mother back to her full health. I remember the agony of feeling helpless, having almost given up hope of her ever regaining complete health.

Mum had always been a very active woman, working most of her married life while raising five children of which I was the eldest. I marvelled at just how hard she worked and how she always appeared to cope while holding the house and family together. Why had this happened to her now at this time of her life? What was the cause? And how could we fix it?

These were just some of the unanswered questions. We realised much later that for some people an illness of this kind can be one of the many catalysts that are used by the higher self to help bring about the inner changes needed for them to begin to look deeper into themselves. For my mother and I, her illness was to be our catalyst into a new life that would be filled with enormous change, growth and satisfaction. It began our spiritual journey into wholeness.

How I found Reiki

Through my hairdressing business I met a woman called Nada Watkins, who was a Reiki Master. On one of her salon visits she commented that I was looking a bit tired. I did feel very flat and drained as my energy was low.

She then gave me some information that intrigued me. She asked me was I aware that while working with people all day, touching them while doing their hair and discussing personal issues with them, that I was giving away some of my personal energy? She continued, "And if that isn't enough ,you then go home to two children, a house and an unwell mother, who all make demands on your time and your energy."

At the time it seemed to me to be a profound statement filled with a lot of truth. Of course, this was not something I didn't know, as you can't do what I did and not suffer some stress. "Yes I know," I replied, but what can I do about it?" I said, feeling this was my lot.

I was aware that as a hairdresser I was listening passively to my clients' hurts and had began to gently counsel them. I felt that it was part of my job to cheer up clients and make them feel better about themselves and life in general. I genuinely cared about them all and, of course, my family, but in doing so I was giving my heart, soul and energy to them. This all made perfect sense to me as I listened to her.

I explained that I was having trouble relaxing and had just begun meditating to help with this. Nada suggested that I might benefit from having a treatment and offered me a healing session with her. I wasn't sure what Reiki was at that time and so my naive reply to this was that I wasn't sick and didn't need healing. She just laughed and said that people don't have to be physically sick or have an illness to have need of the Reiki energy or healing, that it simply would help me to relax mentally and emotionally, similar to what a massage does.

Changed my Life

It was explained to me that Reiki was energy and that healing hands would be placed on specific parts of my body (*mainly energy centres*), and I would be fully clothed. I agreed to have a Reiki healing session the next day. I never told anyone about this at the time.

That healing session changed my life. During the treatment while her hands were on my heart I felt a huge wave of emotion sweeping over me. I began to sob from the depths of my being. I tried to fight it and push it back from wherever it was coming from. I was feeling more than a little awkward, vulnerable and embarrassed, as I was a very private person. With gentle support, reassurance and encouragement I was made feel safe to express this emotion, even though I was not sure where it had come from.

Afterwards, it was explained to me that for a deep hurt to heal properly the suppressed emotions had to surface to be released. It helped me to realise that it was okay to cry and allow this to happen. I had no trouble excepting what was said as it made sense to me. After the crying stopped I felt much lighter and a deep sense of peace crept over me. It was as though I had had all my burdens lifted from me. I left that healing session knowing that something amazing and profound had just taken place. I felt uplifted and my energy levels were normal for the first time in ages.

After that first healing session I was so excited because I had found someone who could help my mother. I told Nada all about my mother's chronic fatigue and she agreed to do a healing on her, but only if Mum wanted to.

Healing My Mother

I was very impressed and told my mother that I thought this woman was a *'real'* healer' and that there was something special about what she did. I made a time and took mum to see her. Nada invited me to participate in my mother's healing session. She explained that the unconditional love that I felt towards my mother would have great healing qualities. Filled with anticipation and excitement I agreed.

I was given a *'mini attunement'* even though I didn't know what that was, which would assist me. I was taken out onto the verandah and seated on a little stool. I was asked to close my eyes and take a few deep breaths and then I was given the attunement.

I remember being filled with warmth and then a white light followed by the colours green and gold flooded my closed eyes. I then experienced a sensation as though the top of my head was opening up and a feeling of tingling. I felt very light and it took only a few minutes. Nothing like this had ever happened to me before. Afterwards I relayed my experiences and was assured that it was all quite normal.

I was given instructions of where to place my hands to assist with my mother's healing. This whole event was nothing short of profound and my mother and I felt a deep sense of mystery and intrigue. We did not feel threatened or unsafe as Nada was full of genuine love, caring and compassion and willingly explained what was happening in terms we could understand. My hands got quite hot and I was over joyed as I saw my mother's face relax for the first time in years.

We had three healing sessions each over the next few weeks. The improvement within my mother was simply amazing. Mum was sleeping better and didn't suffer as much pain.

After these initial healing sessions we were told that we could learn how to do Reiki for ourselves. My mother, in particular, was very interested about this. She had become aware that to learn to cope with chronic fatigue on her own meant that she had to learn how to heal herself. We decided to attend Nada's next Reiki Level One class together. I went mainly out of curiosity and to accompany Mum to be her 'eyes and ears' as her memory was very poor at the time.

We knew absolutely nothing about Reiki other than what we experienced during our healing sessions.

Many people today still stumble across or find Reiki in a similar fashion, not unlike my mother and I. However, there is now much more information available to the general public on the internet.

The fact that my mother and I had not sourced information about Reiki before we experienced it played a huge part in our learning. We simply trusted our personal experiences of the energy as our truth and never thought to question it or doubt that it worked. We had no prejudice or fear; our hearts were open to experience this energy. We accepted that it just worked. In this case ignorance was bliss and worked to our advantage.

There are some things in life that we simply need to experience first-hand before we can have any real understanding. Reiki needs to be experienced to be understood at all. Words simply cannot give the experiences one has while using this energy vibration.

The Journey to Mastership

It was through my connection to our Reiki Master that I was to meet my second husband, Brian. He was a true soul mate, fellow writer and Reiki practitioner. We were married within six months. My mother in the meantime went on to become a Reiki Master through A. J. MacKenzie Clay, who wrote several books about Reiki. Because her own healing had been so amazing she wanted to share it with others. I was so proud of her and revelled in her ability to teach others. I never dreamed that I too, would want this as much as her one day.

Later, I began to get that inner urge to do my Reiki Mastership. At the time I was in denial about any of this. I had to seek inner guidance about it and talked it over with my husband, Brian. Eventually, I completed my mastership under the tutorage and encouragement of my mother, known to many now as Shaman Eilee. It was to be a huge leap in consciousness for me as I embraced the Master's energy.

Through Brian's encouragement my gift of writing began to blossom and my first book, *In Search of Soul*, emerged.

I sold my hair salon and took up full-time teaching, healing and writing. I have been teaching Reiki since early 1997 and currently run seminars and workshops from where ever I am, either in the United Kingdom America or Australia.

Stepping into my Reiki Mastership was to change my husband's and my life and its direction. It opened doors to cosmic consciousness, enabling us both to work with spirit. This I now help teach others about. WpOpening to channel, and working with spirit guides direct for the purpose of healing, or giving psychic readings and spiritual teachings has for me been one of the most rewarding experiences.

I had many interesting experiences as a teacher of Reiki and had no intentions of ever writing a Reiki book, as there were many on the shelves that I felt said enough. However, I found that very few discussed the processes that one goes through while treating oneself with Reiki. Reiki for many is a personal spiritual transformational pathway of which the energy is used simply to gently evolve you.

This path takes the form of transformation through self-healing on all levels of mind, body, emotions and spirit. It allows any negative experiences you have had on any level to gently surface and be released. The more you do this the healthier and happier you and your body become. It's like peeling away layers of a rotten onion to find that the core is still pure and untouched.

Sounds too easy? I believe it is. The only thing that you have to have prior to bringing this about is a genuine commitment to your own healing processes. If you have this, then taking total responsibility for your life will be easier to do. Many start and give up wanting a quick fix to their inner termoil. Nothing is accomplished in life with out dedication and commitment to the practices that work. Reiki is a practice that once you realise how powerful it is, you will want to transform everything, bringing your world and environment into complete balance, experiencing a more positive joyful life.

PART ONE

Why Reiki?

Reiki is a tool sent to help us on our way,
A map to light for the journey today.
The awareness it brings will astound you I'm sure,
As you search for more meaning in this life's tour.
The many revelations of Mind, Body and Soul
Will help you understand that life you can control.
No longer will you feel you are sitting on a shelf
For Reiki will guide you as a teacher of yourself.

Seeking After Wholeness

For a great many years the sense of being whole has been lost in most people. When you watch young children you can see their uninhibited sense of joy, love of life and fearlessness, as their energy seems simply boundless. They obviously still have that wholeness of spirit.

Somewhere along the way to our adulthood, living in our modern culture and busy society we are educated out of this sense of wholeness, the sense that we are one in mind, body and spirit. This way of perceiving ourselves has left us feeling detached, insecure, isolated and disconnected from self and others. It is this sense of being out of touch in some way that leads people to go in search of what seems to be the rest of them. It has been my belief that when society starts to have these problems something turns up to show them how to get back on track. Reiki turns up for many.

Mankind has lost the ability to trust in himself and listen to his instincts. Instead, we have given our power away to the more persistent voices of doubt and reason and peer pressure. We question why something works, rather than accepting that it does, and give thanks something happens instead of giving thanks for what takes place.

It has been during man's search for healing that he has given his own healing processes away. All too often we seek and believe a person with more knowledge of one kind or another must be able to heal us. Sometimes this can work, however, when a healing process does not succeed we still do not seek answers elsewhere. Instead, most people simply accept their condition and get on with coping with it.

It is usually only those considered brave, foolish or desperate to live who question why it is not working and seek out other cures. This is the person who feels deep within them that there must be something else that they can do! This is the one who dares to question and incite others enough to find the answers needed to attain the quality of life available to all. Sometimes this can take a person's lifetime as they pioneer the way for others, such is the path of many a spiritual warrior searching for truth and wholeness of spirit.

Seeking after wholeness is the spiritual warrior's quest, and yet what we are all striving to become by nature is what we find we already are. Becoming conscious of who we really are in essence is what learning Reiki helps to bring about. Learning to accept and express the many parts of us takes courage and wisdom. Quite often we need help in this department.

Reiki has had a profound effect on the lives of thousands of people worldwide, helping to bring them back into wholeness. It is just one of the tools that has been sent to uplift the energy of mankind. Like so many other mysteries of life that cannot really be explained with mere words, so too is the experience of Reiki. This gentle healing energy is hard to explain it needs to be experienced to be believed and understood.

The energy of Reiki moves towards balancing all our energies of mind, emotions, body and spirit, bringing us back into feelings of what can only be called wholeness of self. For many who discover Reiki it will be like coming home and reaching out to turn on the light switch. Through the regular use of Reiki this Inner Light will become brighter and brighter.

What is Reiki?

Reiki (pronounced ray-key) is a Japanese word meaning *rei,* 'universal' and *ki,* 'life–force energy'. There are many other words to describe this same energy found in all cultures. We are all born with this same kind of energy; we call it our living spirit. It is the energy of life itself, that vital life force that flows through all living things. Plants have it, animals have it, our planet, stars, sun and moon have it, and it is the energy that the universe is built on. Reiki is often described as a loving energy, energy with a sense of peace, warmth and security. It makes no difference who is using the energy, love, acceptance and healing is always the end result.

Reiki is not a religion, cult, or organisation. There is no need to change your present belief system. Neither is it a form of mind control, wishful thinking or hypnosis. The practice of Reiki becomes very personal to each individual who learns it. It serves to promote inner growth. As you practice Reiki you will gravitate towards the people and places that will help with that growth.

Reiki was re-discovered by a Japanese man, Dr Mikao Usui, in the mid 1800s. Through study, research and meditations, he evolved a healing system based on ancient Buddhist teachings written in Sanskrit for all peoples. He spent the rest of his life practicing and teaching this method of personal transformation and natural healing which involved attunements to the energy and the laying on of hands. There are many books dealing with the history of Reiki, which has its own controversy, and I do not feel it necessary to cover it here.

This ancient healing art helps to awaken and elevate your own inner energy. During a seminar and through the attunement process you learn how to channel this energy from the universal power within to another person or to oneself, through the use of energising symbols and the laying on of hands. The amount of energy drawn is always determined by the needs of the person receiving it. *(Thy will be done not mine).* It has an innate intelligence of its own governed by universal laws.

There are as many reasons as there are people as to what leads one to the doors of Reiki. There are always catalysts for events that transform our life at any one time. Some of these catalysts have been ill health, depression, longing, curiosity, dissatisfaction, other people, the need for change, and the list goes on. Whatever the reason or catalyst, it is clear to me as a teacher of Reiki that the one thing people seem to forget is the great need we all have to heal and know ourselves. When I speak of healing I don't necessarily mean addressing only sickness. There is healing of past hurts and emotions and of the heart. There is healing of our mind and its habitual negative thinking behaviours.

We spend a great deal of money and time learning about our work or career, our world and all the events that take place within it, when all the while the one very thing that would serve us most we avoid knowing more about, the Self. Self-inquiry and analysis on all levels is what Reiki can help you with, but not necessarily in the conscious mind. True enlightenment can only come when you understand yourself and how you affect everything around you. This helps us take responsibility for all our actions.

When as individuals we can see our lower nature through self-inquiry and accept who we have become as a result of this, we then are faced with the opportunity to change any aspects of ourselves that no longer serve us.

Reiki, therefore, is a spiritual evolving tool that lends a hand by helping us to heal those other parts of us that need assistance. Whether it is in our emotions or our attitudes or our behaviour that needs some adjustment, Reiki can assist us with these adjustments. With each adjustment we see ourselves becoming more whole and accepting who we really are in spirit. As we adjust ourselves and become more whole releasing any negative aspects of self, we feel unburdened and much better. So much so, that this healing process of coming back into wholeness sees people lose aches and pains they have had for years within their physical body. This is the metaphysics of healing; the body is simply the last messenger of the soul.

*Any discomfort within the physical body
is a symptom of an unhappy spirit.*

THE METAPHYSICS OF HEALING

Healing is a term usually saved for the curing of the sick, and generally means getting well. Today, this term means much more and is no longer only reserved for the physically sick or ailing. Our society is beginning to accept that we need to heal many aspects of ourselves to be totally well, not only our physical bodies. People are now seeking counselling for traumas and deep-seated emotional disturbances such as depression or grieving. We are beginning to accept as a people that we have emotions that create some of our physical symptoms, which we experience as unwellness. No longer do we have to wait to get sick before seeking help with a problem. To be part of the solution we must take our life into our own hands and help with our own healing. Healing will only really begin when, as individuals, we accept the responsibility totally for our own health and well-being

VISITING THE DOCTOR

Most people start a healing process by visiting their doctor with symptoms of one kind or another. They receive a physical examination followed closely by tests, a diagnosis, then a prescribed medication or remedy. This is the way we have been taught to cure the physical body and get well. Many people become disillusioned as a result of only treating the symptoms when their illness re-occurs. Doctors become baffled when faced with re-occurring illnesses that cannot be explained or controlled with drugs or operations. The medical profession it seems still chooses to treat us as just a cellular physical body. This type of healing simply doesn't address the whole problem or all the issues involved with healing, for we are more than just a physical body. One baffling illnesses that I personally have come in contact with was my mother's chronic fatigue. For healing to be truly effective it needs to go much deeper than getting rid of physical symptoms in the physical body. Why? Because we are a soul incarnate within our physical body and as such need to realise there are other reasons for becoming ill. The body is the last messenger of the soul, with dis-ease as a last desperate communication from within (higher self) about any negativity or fear, which resides within the heart and mind. We are multi-faceted beings and as such we must treat all these facets when looking at health issues.

Chronic fatigue is a classic result of a suppressed soul trying to illuminate its presence to the conscious mind of the being via the physical body through pain and discomfort. I have found that in most cases of chronic fatigue, while there can be a catalyst of a physical sort helping to exasperate an already tired or ill body, the person suffers foremost with denial of the inner spirit. They are generally suppressed souls unable to rise above the pressures from others to be someone or something that does not serve their highest good. This seems to take place over many years and is a quiet unwellness that slowly creeps over the person. It is because of this fact that most people see it as just a physical problem and rely on the mainstream form of diagnosis from doctors and naturopaths. This helps with some areas of the illness but never quite eradicates it.

Metaphysics is the anatomy of the soul.

LISTEN TO THE BODY

If we set about and try and fix the symptoms of the physical body only, getting rid of the aches and pains, then we dismiss their message to us about ourselves. Our higher self will be trying to tell us in some way that we are not living in harmony within our own belief system. What we do instead is pop a few pills to take away symptoms of discomfort or pain, numbing us, totally ignoring the inner guidance which is telling us to stop and listen to what the body is saying.

How many of you have had a headache only to swallow pain-killing pills to keep on doing whatever it was that you were doing? Headaches are usually a result of stresses and mental/emotional overload. Your body is telling you to stop! Relax and allow the overload to dissipate before you attempt any more. But do we listen?

No! We choose to take control and use a drug that disallows the physical body's message delivered with pain to interfere with the mind's work, of schedules and deadlines and expectations.

> *Medicine is derived from the Latin word medico, which means 'to drug' and has nothing to do with the word 'heal'.*

The body is simply a physical three-dimensional model of your beliefs and thoughts. Your mind is your main computer and it only believes what you tell it, the physical body reacts to the mind's directives. Science has known this for some time but still it is not common knowledge and is not used in the mainstream medical diagnostic process. Until the medical profession recognises quantum physics and brings meta-physics into play with the rest of their medical knowledge, they will still be treating the physical symptoms of a problem and not the ultimate cause.

What is Meant by Metaphysics?

Looking at the metaphysical concepts of disease allows us to understand and discuss alternate ways of looking at the causes of unhappiness or illness. The word *meta* is Latin for 'beyond' and *physics* is 'the physical', so metaphysics simply means beyond the physical. Modern medicine concentrates on the physical body, metaphysics looks beyond the physical, understanding that the mind, emotions, body and spirit are connected as one and works in constant unison and so are never separate.

Over the past hundreds of years the medical profession has seen fit to create a split between the mind and body when treating illness, by treating the physical body only and paying little or no attention to the mind and its emotions or how a patient is feeling. The spirit of the body does not get recognised at all. In ancient times the healers, which were usually priests, viewed their patients as a whole individual. They treated the mind, body and spirit. They knew that only treating part of the person meant that only part of them would get well, resulting in the possible continuation of illness. This was how Reiki was first used in Tibet thousands of years ago.

When we become physically ill it affects our mental and emotional stability, leaving us feeling frustrated and powerless. When we feel unhappy or depressed we usually suffer physically as well, resulting in headaches, muscle tension and nausea. The opposite happens when we feel happy and joyous; our body feels alive, vibrant and healthy.

There is a direct relation between what the mind thinks and how the body reacts.

OUR ENERGY SYSTEM

We are all familiar with the body's main working systems taught to us in science at school. They are: the skeleton, muscles, nervous system circulatory system, digestive system and the endocrine system.

These systems cannot operate without a proper directive from the brain. Our brain is our main computer for life and it is *energy* that runs the brain. Yet, nowhere in Western medicine do we consider the body's energy system. However, most Eastern healing practices have always treated the human energy system along with the physical, fully aware that energy directed from the brain runs our whole body.

Acupuncture, Bowen, Kinesiology, Touch for health, Reiki and massage treat the energy systems of the whole body. They are just some of the alternatives that we have begun to use in our Western healing culture to boost our energy system.

The main cause of imbalance to the energy system begins as some kind of stress! Stress is a direct result of a trauma or negative emotion or experience, mental, emotional or physical that brings discomfort, and it makes no difference whether it is inflicted by you or by someone else.

This stress is received as a shock to one or all of these systems and eventually manifests as dis-ease within the body if it is not seen to. The distress could come from any number of things such as a death, an accident, a relationship breakdown, a frightening experience, exhaustion, chemical poisoning, a dramatic climate change, or bad diet; any negative experience can be responsible. Sometimes it is the subtle emotional stresses that build up over a period of years (which is how I describe chronic fatigue,) eventually becoming along-term negative experience. These are usually things like self-denial, an intimidating husband or parent, an overbearing abusive boss or work colleague, or trying to please everyone at your own expense; the list goes on.

Regardless of the experience it is the cause of the imbalance and is a result of how you reacted to this experience or stress. It is the thoughts you have about the feelings that you have experienced which creates the stress. This stress is then stored within the memory of your own energy field.

Energy imbalances are caused by negative thought patterns due to these stresses, which create the disharmony to your energy. These thoughts are experienced as emotions. Your emotions affect the very fibre of your being; they affect your whole energy system. We are all governed by how we *feel* about the people and events that shape our life, so it is impossible to avoid our emotions. In fact, we need their messages very much.

Of course, many of our emotions are not negative, but it is the negative emotions that go unchecked that create disharmony.

These negative emotional thought patterns may be conscious, as in anger, grief, fear of loss, etc., or they may be subconscious resulting from childhood trauma or fear, long forgotten by the conscious mind. Either way if they are not dealt with they will eventually lead to physical or emotional symptoms of some kind.

Healing Ourselves

My mother suffered chronic fatigue for five years. She went through many specialists and doctors seeking a cure, like anyone else that has had a long-term illness. Many of them told her that she would just have to learn to live with it, as there was nothing they could do. She began to do things for herself. We looked at diet, vitamin and mineral supplements, etc. This helped but nothing significant happened until we eventually discovered Reiki.

Unlike acupuncture, that uses needles to tap into the bodies energy grid, Reiki energy is gently channelled in from the universe through the aura via the chakras (centres of power within our aura), into the physical body and out through the hands. The results of treatments are feelings of warmth and relaxation. Some people go to sleep while having a treatment. What a pleasant way to get well!

My mother began to feel better from the very first time she had a Reiki treatment. After having a few more we decided to learn Reiki for ourselves. While I was not at all physically sick I had some emotional issues that I had been unable to clear within my own mind, so I went along out of curiosity.

My mother's recovery, however, was very swift as she gave herself a treatment daily.

My personal experience with Reiki treatments was different. Feelings that I had suppressed due to long-term fears gently rose and were able to be released without the distress of the emotional attachments. For me, Reiki was a path to inner healing, self-enlightenment and spiritual awakening.

Treats the Cause

The beauty of Reiki is that it treats the cause of distress or illness rather than treating the end result. It balances out the whole energy system so it flows better, bringing harmony back to the physical body through relaxing the mind and emotions and calming the spirit. Reiki enables any negative patterns to surface and be recognised and dealt with safely, removing the cause of the stress.

If you treat yourself often enough you will dissipate all stresses and begin to feel at peace with yourself. It cannot replace medical surgical approaches when needed but it can assist in the recovery and stresses involved.

Popular in Hospitals

Hospital staff, and carers are learning this type of healing and incorporating it in conjunction with their medical background. They recognise its importance in the role of total and complete healing and well-being.

I urge any of you who may be experiencing any distress or discomfort within your lives or bodies to find out about treating your energy system as well as other physical approaches. Learning Reiki for yourself, if you love yourself enough to take the responsibility to begin true healing, is a giant step forward on the road back to wholeness.

The Awakening

As one begins the sacred journey of looking for truth, love and enlightenment an awakening process begins. This awakening sparks unconscious feelings and ideas that urge the inner self to look for answers to many of life's questions. When a person is ready and wants to begin their spiritual journey something usually shows up to help light their pathway. Reiki Level One shows up for many.

There are many reasons why people learn Reiki. Some people are simply curious and want to find out more about metaphysics, while others feel spiritually guided to learn this ancient healing art as part of their healing ministry and to be of service. What they eventually realise is that they are learning Reiki for themselves.

Reiki, first and foremost, is a self-healing modality that has transformational qualities.

Many who learn Reiki are surprised at its simplicity. Learning this ancient healing art simply requires attunements to the energy, the use of ancient symbols and the laying on of hands. It is a vibrational energy-healing tool used for improving health and total well-being by re-balancing our energy system. It is a holistic therapy, which harmonises our body, mind and spirit, using universal energy.

It is so simple even children can learn it. When I first learnt this I wondered why it wasn't taught at schools. You do not have to have any spiritual knowledge or psychic giftedness or be a healer, nor do you have to change your religious beliefs. Reiki is a wonderful tool used for self-development on the journey of self-discovery. For beginners, learning to heal themselves with energy as well as others gives them a great sense of joy and satisfaction, as they see for themselves the changes that can occur.

Many of our natural therapists now incorporate Reiki as one of the modalities used within their practices.

RECHARGE YOUR ENERGY

If you could go home at the end of every hard working day and plug yourself into a socket that would revive your energy levels, wouldn't you want to do it? Of course you would. I use to come home from work feeling exhausted and drained. I first began using Reiki on myself slowly. However, I found that if I gave myself a treatment immediately after work, I had the energy to prepare the evening meal and do other things with my family. It helped me to relax, putting me in a better disposition, especially while interacting with my family, who would normally have to put up with me being a little tired and cranky. Does this sound like you?

My children never interrupted me after I had greeted them and told them I was going to give myself some Reiki. They found that I was a much better person and much more approachable. They, too, use to ask for a Reiki treat if they were not feeling well or happy. My energy level started to increase and I was able to fit more into my day without feeling burnt out at the end of it.

Reiki has always been first and foremost taught in a Level 1 class as a self healing modality.

WHY 'SELF' FIRST?

There is probably no other method of self-treatment as simple and as effective as Reiki. There are many healing modalities that are great but cannot be applied to self. You can give yourself a treatment wherever you are, because after receiving the attunements Reiki is always with you. By simply placing your hands on your body you will receive the energy, no other devices are necessary. You do not have to be unclothed or use special oils. The Reiki self-treat is a technique which, when used often, will transform and enhance your life. The more you treat yourself the more you build up and restore your body and the more energy you will possess.

When I was first taught we were told that we must draw from the well of Reiki first to nourish and give to ourselves, for there will always be more than enough to nourish others. I find that many people who learn Reiki want to use it purely to heal others. That is okay and noble, but we must all learn to heal ourselves first. We can never really heal others; we can only be of assistance to them. We can only ever heal ourselves.

We have but one temple in this universe and that is of our own body. It is with love and personal responsibility of the self that we need to give Reiki to ourselves first before giving it to others. The need for more personal healing sees many learning how to do this through the use of Reiki.

What You May Experience

Many people begin whole new lives when they learn Level One Reiki. Not in the physical sense but in the more personal and spiritual sense. They become aware of an energy that they never knew existed. For some this energy represents their first conscious understandings of Spirit or God. Reiki is just one of the energies of the Divine. It is gentle and warm and non-threatening, and helps bring about a feeling of wholeness and completeness.

The attunement process at this stage allows the whole energy field to undergo an energy shift on all subtle levels, which over a period of time, settles into the denser layers of energy within the conscious mind and physical body. This marks the beginning of a series of events I call awakenings unto the true nature of self and self-healing. Students are not usually aware of this happening as it can be very subtle, but it happens nonetheless.

The Reiki One workshop is the first of its kind for some people. They have no idea what is about to transpire for them and are not quite sure why they have attended. It has always been clear to me that when a pupil is ready, a teacher will be found, and so it is with the learning of this energy. The higher self of a student demands that it is time to learn more about self on all levels.

It has always amused me when students say they are attending a Reiki workshop for the benefit of someone else. However, this is not always the case in the end. Even highly spiritually evolved people are amazed at the processes that attunements help to bring about for them.

NEW CONCEPT FOR MANY

The concept of energy for those who have never studied science or metaphysics before is always new, and learning its dynamics is a whole new experience. What they discover is that humans are consciousness energy beings, vibrating at different frequencies all the time, a part of all living energy but individual by nature.

I found this to be a hard concept to grasp at first, but I knew that when I treated myself with Reiki something wonderful happened to me. This acknowledged experience helped me to go beyond my conscious beliefs and accept that some things just work and that I didn't need to know any more.

Reiki One brings with it a renewed sense of responsibility to self. For many this is hard to accept at first and so it can bring with it some discomfort as the acceptance process takes time to integrate. Others find the concept of healing oneself challenging the very fabric of their belief system as they have been so use to running off to doctors for whatever ailed them. We have been programmed to believe that our healing process lies in the hands of others and not our own. Reiki One helps people go beyond this type of rigid belief, allowing them to assist in their own healing processes simply by using Reiki energy.

Dr Usui realised he had to bring spirituality into his teachings and developed the five spiritual principals of using Reiki. We need to understand that Reiki is not just another healing modality. Besides being a balancing and restoring energy technique, it is also a transformational force for personal growth. If we act in accordance with these principles, they help give us a moral foundation and provide us with a more philosophical outlook to life, ultimately helping to lead us to more spiritual enlightenment.

The Five Spiritual Principals

1. Just for today I will let go of worry.
2. Just for today I will let go of anger.
3. Just for today I will love and respect all forms of life.
4. Just for today I will accept my many blessings.
5. Just for today I will live my life honestly.

During the course of learning in Level One Reiki, one would expect to find out the concept of energy in relation to the self and to the healing process of oneself. An understanding of the aura and related chakras should also be taught to help appreciate the energy. Along with the history and spiritual principals of Reiki, Level One usually takes two to three days to complete. This gives time for the attunement process to begin working and allows the student enough time to ask relevant questions and gain the answers.

Many of my students in the Level Two class tell me that after completing Level One they noticed some interesting changes with the way other people treated them. One of my more sceptical students was told that she looked 10 years younger by a friend who hadn't seen her for a while. My student was so thrilled by this that she enrolled in the next Level Two course.

Level One students tell me of similar experiences but find it difficult to explain to their friends about the energy. They have yet to bridge that gap of worrying about what other people will think when confronted with something new.

Part of the Level One process is learning to stand firm in what you know to be your truth. It does not matter if your truth threatens someone else's as long as it is spoken with love, then it just is. Your experiences with Reiki and life are just that – yours. The other person's reaction to this is just that, their reaction. As long as you are happy with your truth and don't feel the need to defend it or justify it, they will actually sense that what you have said is obviously true for you. Unsure, they may ask more questions or leave it till a later date. Either way, there is a growth step taken when we learn to slowly pull away from the expected mass beliefs and accept that our own experiences are our truth, no matter how obscure they may seem to others.

This is the experience many Reiki One's go through. I found it difficult talk to anyone about Reiki when I first learnt it. I feared that I would be judged as wrong, silly or crazy. I wasn't strong enough within myself at that time to tackle any confrontation to do with this newfound self-healing.

As I treated myself more and more, I settled into an understanding of how I felt and just what this energy could do for me. The energy helped me to accept my truth of it without the need for approval from others.

I realised too that I was pulling away from group or tribal consciousness to do with the excepted norm. I could not go back to my old beliefs and had to trust my new ones based on my experiences of how the energy worked. I find that this kind of acceptance happens to everyone to some degree when they accept that it is okay to treat themselves with Reiki. It does work.

COMING HOME

Learning Reiki feels like coming home. This home is usually their heart. The heart is where we connect to the soul and to our spiritual nature. From here we begin to realise that our connection is with the whole universe. Connecting at this level within self sees great personal transformations begin to take place. Most often the first level takes people who are devoid of self-love straight to their own heart for healing.

The heart is where we reconcile with our perceptions of unconditional love, especially of the self. People have generally been seeking love externally believing it exists outside of themselves through, probably, numerous failed careers and relationships. What they find is that each love just doesn't meet with their preconceived expectations, or their career only helps to emphasise their own lack of self worth. They usually have an unrealistic ideal as to what love is, especially self-love. So all the heart issues to do with learning about unconditional love are brought to the surface. Connecting with the heart helps to heal all our relationship issues by bringing them to the surface. The heart is the pathway to the soul. To connect at this level we must all travel our heart lessons and come back into wholeness learning to love self first.

Many reconnect with nature at this time, being that Mother Earth is our most supreme mother who loves us all unconditionally. The heart helps us connect to nature, which is quite often a big catalyst for healing in the truest sense of the word. You rarely leave a trip into nature as stressed as when you arrived. Green, the colour of nature is also the colour of our heart chakra.

Self Discovery

Most students, if they haven't begun searching for more information about themselves, who they are and where they fit into the big scheme of things, seem to begin the process of seeking more knowledge about self after Level One. Certain informative books just seem to find their way to us when we need them. Whatever we need to know just miraculously rocks up.

The universe acts in accordance with our thoughts and resonates to our requests like a delivery clerk, that is if we are clear about what it is we want to know or experience. So when the question is asked the answer turns up, sometimes in the most unusual ways. Learning to be open to how the universe converses with us is part of the process of Level One energy. Being able to see a bigger picture of things helps bring comfort in our pressured and stressful world.

Many Level One students become so enthralled with their own healing process that they want to learn more and see that true healing must take place on all levels for it to be effective. More of the metaphysical aspects of healing are quite often pursued after learning Level One. Many may never do Level Two but move on to use their energy within other healing fields. I find that learning Reiki One opens doors to the soul and its true purpose. For some this is all they require to catapult them into their soul's pursuits for this lifetime. In this manner I have found that Reiki is one of the fastest means to accessing our soul's identification.

For others it is a matter of personal healing that brings them to Reiki in the first place. These people seem to go through a great ordeal of unlearning, like peeling away layers of an onion. Such is the process of healing for those who use Reiki as a means to access the hidden things that have seen them become unwell. For them the practice of Reiki is like a ritual that they need to do every day without fail.

Some of the healing results that they have achieved are simply awesome. The power of personal healing and transformation that comes from taking charge of self through the process of Reiki is something that has to be felt to be believed. Those who have travelled this path become our Reiki Master/Teachers, as they know only too well the benefits they have received from learning it first hand. They teach their healing experiences from the heart and their honesty is felt as truth by their fellow students. They make powerful teachers of Reiki.

The more advanced or evolved people who come to a Level One class experience a different process. Some of my more advanced Level One students find that Reiki puts everything together for them within a working modality and concept that they can use as a bridge to their clients.

Many natural therapists, such as naturopaths, use Reiki to assist with healing their clients. Counsellors use Reiki for helping them counsel. For other advanced students it marks the beginning of their journey with spirit. They are reconnected to the Divine during an attunement and for some this helps to connect them to guides and angels whom they are going to be working with.

Some of these students may already be adept psychics but have not yet been able to deal with their own heart issues or come to terms with their innate gifts. Sometimes when there are changes with our spirit guides the attunements can help realign the energies of mind, body and spirit, bringing back balance.

Wholeness is the result of the attunement process, so it does not matter at what level this needs to occur.

The Attunement Process

The attunements are a very personal experience for each student. As each new student receives their attunements they can experience many different emotions and feelings. Some see colours, feel sensations, visit a past life or see a spirit guide. Others feel teary or joyful and even giggly. It is an individual experience, one that I always like to share with my students afterwards. In Reiki One there is four attunements; two on the first day of the seminar and two on the second day.

After receiving the attunements there are usually some changes. The first thing most notice is that their hands will usually get warm most times when they place them on themselves or another person. Often, students will get energy surges coming from their hands; this is quite natural as they are now a Reiki channel.

These changes will happen over a few days or weeks and because of this we encourage all level one students to have a Reiki self-treat everyday for 21-30 days after. This is part of a cleanse or shift and helps them integrate the new knowledge by using the Reiki energy.

Reiki One helps to clear auras of uninvited influences and gives a sense of peace and calmness back to the students.

Some students, during either an attunement or simply during a meditation, may have visualisations of the spiritual kind take place for the first time. This can be all part of their first awakening to the energies of the Divine and to spirit.

I am very aware that no matter what happens for each individual student they all receive exactly what they are requiring to take place at that time for their highest good and healing. It is worth remembering at this point that nothing ever takes place on a spiritual plane without the permission from the higher self.

A Reiki Master can only be a facilitator for part of the learning, how and what you choose to take from his/her teachings will be up to you as a student. There are so many different levels of consciousness out there in teaching Reiki Masters that it is impossible to expect us all to be the same or teach the same way.

Other Benefits

On a more physical level, learning Level One helps students with everything from broken bones, speeding up surgery recovery, childbirth, asthma to eschma, to healing depression, and a broken heart.

Life can see many people go through the healing processes mentioned above. However, Reiki gently moves people through their own healing processes on all levels at their own pace without the need to experience the pain. It generally speeds up what would normally take a long time to transpire. As people treat themselves with Reiki they move one more step closer to that wholeness of self and of spirit. This is why Reiki is a healing teacher first and foremost of self through our journey of life.

Reiki for me has been a Rite of Passage, initiating me into deeper understandings of who I am on all levels, illuminating just what that means to me.

Level One took me into my heart and helped me to discover and connect with the universal unconditional love that I had been seeking in my life. It re-connected me to Divine love so that, finally, I could see how this energy worked and lived in all things. No longer was I to feel lonely as my soul connected with that of others. The people and places I was meant to grow and learn from were presented to me as I moved more and more into self-acceptance. Much of it I did not fully understand.

On reflection I could see for myself the changes that had taken place within me. Level One is an awakening process, an awakening of the Divine essence that is in all things, an awakening of one's soul self.

The Healing Touch

In Level One we teach basic fundamentals such as the power of touch. Touch is the first experience when we come out of the womb and into the world. From then on we like that sensation; it represents life to us. Babies can die from lack of touch and so do relationships.

Researchers from the University of Wisconsin took baby monkeys from their mother at birth and raised them separately in cages. They were deprived of touch, resulting in severe neurotic behaviour and, in some cases, death. Research has also shown that physical touching is just as essential for human infants.

Our sense of touch is a powerful communicator. It soothes us, comforts us, encourages us, excites us, or enrages us. It is a means of expression for love, warmth, affection, understanding, approval, acceptance, or alternatively anger, fear, insecurity, or rejection. To touch is a natural reaction or instinct.

When we hurt ourselves we hold or rub the injured area. It instantly makes it feel better. When children are emotionally hurt we hug them until they feel better, holding them close so they can feel loved, accepted and secure. Adults, too, need this kind of support when feeling low or emotionally injured. However, they worry about rejection and quite often don't ask for this kind of support. We also touch out of happiness and love but, more often than not, only by family members and close friends.

As physical beings we need touch! In Western and Eastern society we have so many taboos relating to touching. Who we touch, where we touch each other, and can we be seen touching each other? Touching seems to evoke a great many thing in most people, however, it seems we have lost contact with those feelings. The skin is the largest organ of the body and scientist still cannot duplicate it with all its complexities. It is our largest sense organ and is extremely sensitive, letting us know if we feel hot, cold, pleasure or pain.

Without the physical contact there is a feeling of emptiness, an inner craving, or hunger which food cannot satisfy. When we were babies and were held, loved, cuddled and stroked, there was no doubt as to our being touched or loved. We knew we could get a cuddle from Mum or Dad and other family members when we needed it. As we grew up it seems that we were touched less and less. While growing up we are encouraged to seek independence and for some reason that means less physical contact. It seems that touching represents either some weakness or unnecessary familiarity.

It is no wonder that many healing modalities are based on touch, such as massage, shiatsu, Rolfing, pulsing, Feldenkrais, kinesiology and Reiki, just to name a few. Some people confuse hugging or touching with sex. A misunderstanding that causes people who fear sex to avoid hugging. Others are led into a life of sexual promiscuity when all they really need is a hug. Sex and hugging are two different things.

Through my Reiki seminars students are invited to rediscover the joy and healing and loving that nurturing touch can bring about, not only to yourself, but also to others.

Hugging is good for you!
Did you receive a hug today?
Did you give someone a hug today?
Four hugs a day keeps the doctor away!
Eight hugs for Maintenance!
Twelve hugs for Growth!

Pranic Breathe Activation

Breathing helps the mind and body relax and is the easiest way to teach simple meditational techniques. Because of this I teach Pranic breathing to all my Level One students, helping them to relax and feel their attunements better.

Breathing is the first miracle of life itself, a magical process, a sign of being alive. Of all the things our body needs to survive, breath is the most critical. We can go without food and water for days if necessary but we cannot go without breathing for more than a few minutes.

Breathing is our truest expression of the life force flowing through us, eventually to all our organs and tissue sustaining every cell in our body. We take this action for granted. You don't have to think about breathing, it just happens. It's programmed into your living DNA and genetic memory as a reflex to life.

In some Eastern cultures the way people breathe is taken very seriously but Western society pays little or no attention to it at all, unless you are drawn to meditation classes, yoga, Tai Chi or other such disciplines. Most of the time our breath flows in and out of our body of its own accord and in its own rhythm. It isn't until you do some strenuous exercise or have a shock or trauma that its rhythm is upset and you take notice of it.

When we become aware of our breath and learn to develop the habit of breathing deeply, filling our lungs full, then exhaling completely, we can experience new levels of awareness. You are taught to concentrate on the breath when you begin to meditate by concentrating your whole awareness on breathing – the in-breath through the nostrils, then the out-breath through the mouth or nose – following it into your diaphragm as it expands with the in-breath. Stress and all emotional dross and mental baggage can be left behind with each deep breath you take. This is the reason most people learn to do short meditations concentrating on the breath, which helps to keep them calm. Think of a sigh; it releases tension through the breath.

Now, notice how you are breathing. You might be a shallow breather by only filling the upper part of the chest, or maybe you breathe filling your lungs to find your tummy expanding with each breath. Try deep breathing and send your breath to a point at the navel. This will help you to deep breathe.

Deep breathing is important, especially during the opening and closing of an attunement process. I encourage my students to be aware of their breathing throughout my seminar, and they are pleasantly surprised at the benefits it brings.

When to Do Your Self-Treat

For the best results self-treats are done on a daily basis. It should be made into a special time of the day; a ritual that you set aside just for you. Most people put themselves last, giving to everyone else first, and only if there is time left over do they give to themselves.

This is an opportunity for you to claim some personal space, and it is an act of self-love. Most people have found that with consistent Reiki self-treats their energy increases; their self confidence grows; tiredness diminishes, and their knowledge of self expands as they feel much better within themselves. This helps benefit everyone else around you as well as yourself.

A full Reiki self-treat takes about an hour. It can be done first thing in the morning in bed before you get up to take a shower, or last thing at night (if you fall asleep, that's okay) or any other time during the day that suits you. During a self-treat most people feel relaxed as it dissipates anxiety, some reach a deep meditative state, so it is best not to break the flow during the hour.

A self-treat is equivalent to about 2-3 hours good sleep.

I have found that Reiki helps with many problems, especially emotional ones and gives people the energy they need to think with more clarity. It helps most people come to terms with their heart's lessons about unconditional love, which is why I now teach this wonderful healing art. Moving into the heart and healing its many hurts does much on the road to personal healing.

Many of my students report very similar feelings. One lady said she stopped yelling at her son for weeks after her Level One class, to the relief of them both. While others say that they feel more at peace within themselves. It can be life changing as they discover that there is more to the human energy experience than they ever knew before.

Here are a few areas in which the use of Reiki has been helpful: Relieving pain and discomfort from chronic diseases, promoting recovery from surgery, headaches, colds, flu, cuts, burns, fatigue, stomach upsets and sprains, etc., emotional upsets, replenishing of depleted energy, reducing stress and tension, enhancing personal expression and creativity, and helping to change outmoded belief systems and releasing negative feelings about people and past experiences.

Here are some of the self-treat positions taught during a Level One seminar. All positions are held for about five minutes each.

Head Positions

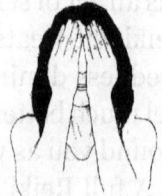

Position 1.
Cover the eyes and front of the face with tips of fingers touching the hairline, or forehead.

Position 2.
Place hands over side of the head, either over the ears or just above them, with tips of the fingers touching at the crown.
Keeping the fingers gently closed. An alternative position is placing the hands over the ears.

Position 3.
Place hands horizontally behind the head. One hand above the occiput ridge, or base of the scull, the other just below it.

Position 4.
One hand is placed around the throat gently resting on the chest, while the other hand is below on the upper chest.

FRONT POSITIONS

Position 1.
Place hands over both breasts or chest with middle fingers touching.

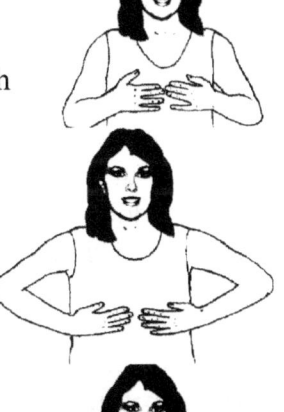

Position 2.
Hands are placed over the lower rib cage on either side of the body with fingers touching in the centre, above the waist.

Position 3.
Place hands below the waist, on each side of the body, fingers touching in the middle of your abdomen.

Position 4.
Place hands together over the pubic bone pointing towards your feet, thumbs touching.

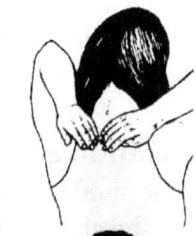

The back positions

Position 1.

Reach up and place hands on your neck and shoulder muscles, with the middle finger tips touching the spinal column.

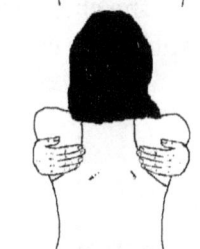

Position 2.
Cross your arms in front of you, hugging yourself, resting your hands on the shoulder blades.

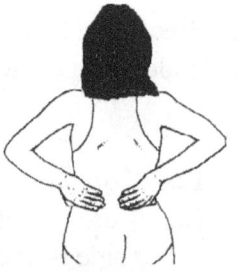

Position 3.
Place your hands at your waistline at the back, with middle fingertips on the spine and thumbs on the waistline.

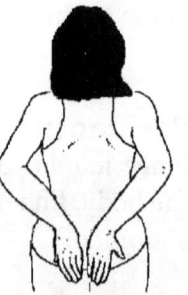

Position 4.
Place your hands over the lower buttocks with fingers pointing downwards and meeting at the tailbone.

Other positions you may try

Position 1.
Front and back of both ankles.
Do both ankles.

Position 2.
Place hands on front of both knees together.
Then do the back of knees

Position 3.
Knee and ankle done together.
One hand on the knee the other
on the ankle. Do both legs.

Position 4.
The base of one foot with the
hand either side of the foot.
Or do both feet.

Level 1 Symbology

Symbols are where metaphysics meets spirituality, or God and science combine for the greater good of all. I teach basic symbology during Level One Reiki. This would probably be met with some controversy from the traditional sectors of Reiki, as they seem to teach symbology with trepidation and some fear. I do not have any such fears nor do I like to project such negativity onto new initiates. It is incorrect to believe that which is sacred should also be kept secret. There are no secrets in the universe. It is the symbols of Reiki that sets it apart from all other healing modalities. Symbology has an esoteric quality and deals with the basis of all real metaphysics.

Dr Usui discovered these symbols and understood that they were a means to accessing the hidden wisdom of universal energy for healing. The symbols are the key to unlocking the energy. Reiki symbols help us to manifest an otherwise unrealised energy, and this part of the Reiki concept, I feel, needs to be taught up front during Level One. Most traditional teachings do not teach any symbols until Level Two.

Symbols were used long before written language was invented. Nature expresses itself through symbols. We see symbolic designs in the centre of flowers, trees, shells and rocks. Symbols are a language beyond language, as well as information with significance.

Think about the thought transference that takes place upon viewing a symbol. All the symbols used in our society today, for road signs, chemical warnings and danger, are universal in their application. Even the simple toilet symbol or the arrow is universal in application. We register them on a subconscious level. Symbols act as a map to the inner self of higher consciousness. It is much faster than the slower process of conscious thoughts or the written or spoken word. Some symbols can be likened to a puzzle, which holds specific hidden knowledge like the ancient Mayan or Egyptian hieroglyphics.

Reiki symbols help unlock our subconscious and conscious mind to experience the energy. When you focus the mind on these symbols and their purpose, your intent lines up with the energy as it flows. So in this way the symbols focus the mind on the purpose of this energy, helping you to increase its flow.

Each symbol has a particular purpose and therefore has its own vibrational energy. Upon using the symbols the practitioner becomes aware of the energy it generates. Remember, the energy generated from any symbol is dependent on the intent and focus of your mind. Use your breath to clear your mind and then focus your intent before you use them. We ask you all to respect them and use them wisely for the betterment of yourself and others and all life forms.

The Divinity symbol – 'Let go – Let God'

This symbol represents forgiveness and protection. It has been in use for centuries and will be familiar to you. Its importance during Reiki is to assist in the releasing process of energy blockages within the receiver (let go – let God). It brings gifts of forgiveness and generates more acceptance of the flow of life helping with the emotional fears of change. It can also be used for the protection from negative energy. This is a powerful symbol when used on the feet for grounding after a treatment; it is also the symbol for earth in astrology.

The Cho-ku-rei symbol
– 'All the power of the universe unites' This symbol represents the spiralling of the life-force energy and is the key to the energy and brings with it an acceptance of the experience of change. Hence, its great importance in the healing process with Reiki. It is used at the beginning of channelling activating the energy 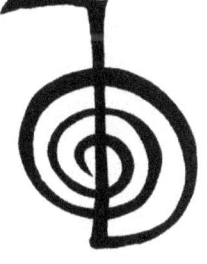 and also used over the chakras. Do not be hesitant in using this symbol for it can do no harm. You cannot overdose on Reiki.

The Tam-a-ra-sha symbol
– 'A shift in a Consciousness'
This symbol represents the passing of one level of understanding to a higher level. Its importance during Reiki is to allow the receiver's mind to explore its full potential. Used on the 'third eye' it instigates movement from the material or physical realm to the spiritual realms of  understanding. This symbol is excellent for use on people with recurring illness or an issue they are having trouble with on a conscious level. It is also good to use also when meditating, helping to take you to a higher consciousness within. It also can be used on the feet for grounding. You must have clear intent as to the purpose of the symbols as you use them.

Reiki Prayer

Before we begin any Reiki healing it is important to put it in the right context, so a small prayer helps us to bring in the right vibration. In this little prayer you will notice that the healing is handed over to the higher self of the person who is receiving the healing. As Reiki channels we are simply instruments who facilitate the healing; it comes through us rather than from us.

This is the basic principal of channelling energy for healing self or others. You may like to use this prayer for your own healing sessions.

A Reiki Prayer

Mother, Father, God,
Thank you for the gift of Reiki,
Thank you for allowing me to be a clear
channel for the Reiki healing energy.
I now ask that my higher self
Communicate all that is necessary
for my highest good,
At this time in this place,
So Be It.

How to Treat Others

Treating others will give you great joy, but there are some things to remember. Firstly, a person must ask to have a treatment. It is not correct if you are the only one wanting to treat them; they must want to have a treatment. Secondly, there needs to be an exchange for the service to keep respect and honour. It doesn't necessarily mean accepting money as payment. An exchange of services is fine or a gift or donation if that is okay with you. This is because most people do not place value on something they get for free and many do not expect it to be free. Giving something without an exchange can create an obligation, and the person may never come again.

I have swapped Reiki treats for essential oils, bath salts, crystals, books, clothing and labour. It doesn't matter what the exchange is but there must be one. Well-being has value and ultimately the exchange reflects a feeling of worthiness to both the giver and receiver. It is an act of self-love from the person who wishes to receive Reiki. It should be an honourable exchange, done with love.

The Healing Environment

This should reflect a feeling of peace and comfort. A healing environment should feel inviting and relaxing. Not too clinical, but hygienically clean with fresh towels on the massage table. Soft relaxing music is pleasant as are flowers and crystals. Some comfortable soft pillows for the head and under the knees and ankles helps. Burning incense or essential oils clears the atmosphere and helps to create a feeling of tranquillity.

When conducting a Reiki treat for someone, even if it's at home, make it a peaceful experience for the person receiving it. Lawn mowers and chainsaws are distractions, so are children shrieking in the background. So try to arrange a time when all is quiet. I like to have some fresh cold water handy. After a treatment you will both feel a little dry, and it's a great time to chat about the treatment.

The Treatment

Most treatments are carried out on a massage table, as they are comfortable and portable. If there is not a place for the person to lie down then a chair will do. It is preferable for the recipient to lie on their backs – without footwear – with the head resting on a cushion or pillow and something similar placed under the knees for added comfort. Jewellery and watches should be removed as this can interfere with the energy. Have a dish handy for these items to be put safely into. If it is cool, a cover could be used for added warmth. Feet and hands can get cold. It is well known that when we relax our breathing slows down and our body temperature drops by a few degrees.

For ease of movement make sure that the table you are working on has plenty of room around it. You may like to sit on a small chair with castors so you can move freely as you give Reiki. I always begin any healing session with a prayer. I do not always say it out loud. This aligns my higher self without ego and puts the right vibration in place at the very beginning of the treatment. Then I visualise the symbols and begin the session.

We begin at the four head positions. Place yourself at the head where it is comfortable to sit. Some people like to talk while they receive Reiki and others drift off into sleep. Whatever happens it is advisable that the talking comes from them and not you. It is okay to answer back when spoken to, however, it is more beneficial for them if they rest and relax. Reiki is a personal experience so let people experience it how they wish.

I like to explain the treatment to first-time clients, which helps to put them at ease. I tell them to just relax and enjoy the session and have a talk afterwards. I then give them Reiki as I would give it to myself with only a few adjustments to hand positions.

All head positions are carried out standing or sitting behind the person receiving. It is much easier and more comfortable for both of you. During the time I am healing I tend to use my pranic breathing as this helps me to channel more easily. This can take quite some practice and is not necessary for beginners; however, you may like to try it. At the end of each healing I always sweep the aura in circular motions or in a figure of eight. I release myself from the person's aura, giving thanks for the healing that has just taken place while handing them back into the care of the Creator.

FRONT POSITIONS

Position 1.
Stand behind the person placing hands over the eyes (third eye chakra), gently cupped covering the nose as well. The heel of hand should be at the hairline.

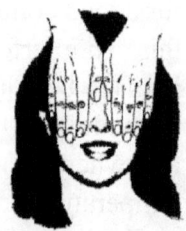

Position 2.
Gently place one hand either side of the head with the little finger resting above the ears. It can also be done over the ears.

Position 3.
Gently place cupped hands, palms up under-neath the head. This position covers the occipital ridge (third eye chakra). The healer does the lifting.

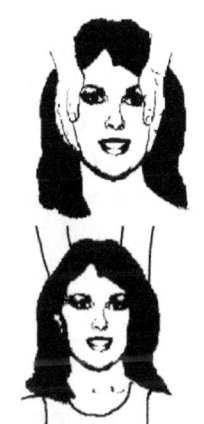

Position 4.
Place hands over the collar bone covering the throat chakra. An alternative position is to rest one hand over the throat and the other hand slightly overlapping it over the chest.

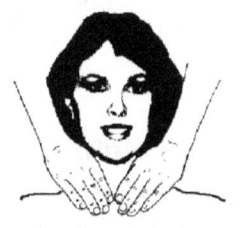

Position 5.
Place both hands on the chest in a T formation covering the heart chakra. With males both hands can be placed across the chest in a similar hand position to that shown alternatively.

Position 6.
Place hands below the breasts over the solar plexus chakra. The heel of one hand should touch the middle finger of the other hand.

Position 7.
Both hands are placed across the pelvic area, just below the navel over the sacral chakra.

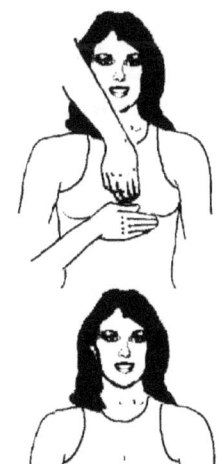

Position 8.
Place the heel of one hand just above the pubic bone and the other hand placed in the opposite direction in the creases of the thighs.
This position covers the base chakra.

BACK POSITIONS

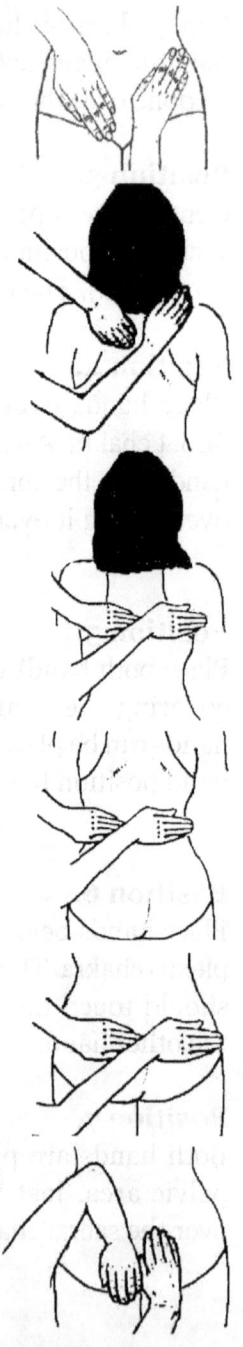

Position 1.
Place both hands on the shoulders muscles either side of the neck.

Position 2.
Both hands are placed, one in front of the other, over the shoulder blades.

Position 3.
Move down the back, one hand width, to cover the kidney area.

Position 4.
Place hands on the lower back below the waist, over the sacrum.

Position 5.
Place hands together, one towards the head and the other hand pointing towards the feet over the coccyx (tailbone).

Practical Applications

As a Reiki Master it never ceases to amaze me just how many different ways we can use the energy of Reiki. This life-force energy is found in every living thing, so it can be used on everything in numerous ways. Once you have been attuned to this energy you have a survival kit like no other. Here are some simple every day uses for the Reiki energy.

Cleansing and Clearing

All areas or rooms give off energy and so have an energy vibration. One of the most practical ways to use Reiki energy is for the cleansing of rooms or specific areas.

Have you ever walked into a room where you could cut the air with a knife? You can use the energy of Reiki to clear and recharge an area with the use of energising Reiki symbols, which vibrate at perfect harmony and balance. This has the effect of clearing the atmosphere of any negative influences and filling it with more harmonious vibrations. Great if things are not feeling good at work or home. It's a pleasant thing to do if you are preparing a room for something special.

In the same manner Reiki can be used for the clearing and the recharging of crystals and wands used for healing or to create ambience. By clearing and treating minerals such as crystals or precious stones and jewelry they effectively become an added positive source of energy when you wear them.

Personal Protection

In a very similar manner you can use the Reiki energy to clear your own aura of uninvited influences and create a protective barrier around you, helping to ward off otherwise energy parasites. Using some of the basic Reiki symbology you are programming you own energy field not to take on board other people's negative energy. Reiki is the energy of love and fear and love cannot coexist, so the more one uses the energy of Reiki the more you build up an energy protective screen to other people's fear that is felt as negativity. Reiki can also be used to clear the auras of loved ones.

Reiki First Aid

The energy of Reiki is always going to be with you once you have been attuned. You will always have your hands you, so you will have a first aid kit with you all the time. During the course of a day there will be many time that calming hands can help you and your colleagues if they wish it. Stress is our biggest problem. The pressure to finish on time, make deadlines and compete professionally all take the fun out of work. Simply placing your hands on your solar plexus and the heart and taking a few deep breaths will be enough to help you gather your energy.

Reiki aids in accidents and can be of assistance to calming people who have suffered shock or trauma. It has also been known to help in the slowing down of blood flow from injuries. Of course, medical first aid should also be applied. Reiki is very effective with little children when small hurts occur and reassurance is needed.

Insect bites and sprains can be relieved within a few minutes. It often helps to keep swelling down to a minimum. The same can be said for bruising. Many burns have been known to not hurt anywhere near as much after applying Reiki for a while. If you can give Reiki to a burn immediately then blisters are less likely to appear.

More often than not Reiki is best used for the effects of trauma and shock if used on the heart and solar plexus, helping to bring breathing back to normal and allowing calm to replace fear.

Gadgets

All things consist of vibrating energy patterns, even dense objects. Reiki can be used for just about anything that you can think of, such as watches, batteries, all kinds of machines and gadgets that won't work; so why not try Reiki on them? It has been know to work on jammed locks, doors and windows. The car battery is something else you may like to try Reiki on when it is flat and won't start.

Food Preparation

People who are attuned to Reiki are able to put the life force back into their food while they prepare it. It helps to increase its nutritional value. With all the chemicals and additives that are placed in our foods nowadays this is a great way to neutralise it. By using the Reiki symbols and placing your hands over food for a short while you are able to increase the energetic level and help to cleanse it by changing its vibrations. It is usually a good idea to Reiki all food if you are not preparing it yourself, e.g., restaurants. It comes in handy if you are travelling and are concerned about hygiene. When you Reiki the food you are thanking the creator for the bounty of Mother Earth and this is a good practice.

Many people who take medicines also Reiki their prescribed medication, creating perfect harmony and balance so that there will be very little side effects. The possibilities are now becoming endless. A company I know of uses Reiki to add the vibration to their natural healing products.

Meditation

If, like me, you find it hard to meditate at first, then the use of Reiki is a marvellous tool for meditation. The mind goes straight in to an alpha state when Reiki is applied. It is this is a more relaxed state and helps us to be calm.

As we calm and our body relaxes it is easier to obtain the mental state for meditation. Most people find that with continual use of Reiki they are able to relax their mind and so begin to meditate during treatments. It becomes natural.

Reiki helps put us in touch with that core of ourselves, being our soul. With the use of symbols we are able to bring more awareness to our meditations. We can feel much lighter as we learn to raise our levels of vibration. This has the effect of also raising our consciousness, helping us to observe our thoughts and feelings. Through this type of observation and awareness we become aware of the adjustments we may need to make to our attitudes about life or our beliefs about ourselves. We can experience our spiritual selves more and more during our Reiki treatment and this helps us to adjust our levels of knowledge about oneself. We can discover who we really are and find more purpose to life.

Plants and Animals

The life force energy exists within plants and animals alike and they respond very well to Reiki. Plants have been known to come back to life when they are on their last legs when given regular treatments. Hold your hands around the roots of the plant or the base of the pot for about 10 minutes every day and see the results for yourself. Try it on your vegetable patch or seedlings; you'll be amazed at the results.

Our dog, Charlie, always comes for a Reiki treatment when she is feeling a little low. A friend's dog, Ben, came over to me and put his head into my hands. He had an accident, which resulted in 20 stitches in his head and was in a lot of pain. The owners were amazed because he knew exactly where to go for relief and healing.

Animals are treated in much the same way you treat humans. By placing your hands at various body positions you note how much energy they seem to be drawing. Cats and birds love Reiki when it is given and will quite often seek you out for it. Many vets and veterinary nurses are learning Reiki as a calming tool for their treatment of sick animals. It hastens the recovery from anaesthetic or drugs. Animals, like humans, can suffer anxiety when they are ill or in strange surroundings, so calming Reiki hands can help.

Massage and Other Therapies

There are many therapies that can be used with Reiki. Massage is very common. Therapists are able to use this universal life-force energy and not their own energy when massaging. They are less physically fatigued by the exertion and are usually energised by the Reiki energy instead.

The client receiving the massage is able to relax more deeply, helping the massage to work better in reducing muscular as well as mental and emotional stress.

When incorporating Reiki with other therapies it usually has the added effect of helping that therapy to work better on all levels of mind, body, emotion and spirit instead of just one or two. From the therapist's point of view it helps them on an intuitive level by enabling them to tune into their client's needs, thereby enhancing their healing. Reiki is of great benefit to natural therapists on a practical level as well as a personal one.

COUNSELLING

Reiki is very effective when used for counselling, whether they are clients, work colleagues, friends or family. Firstly, it helps calm those needing to express feelings that they are not sure of. It creates an atmosphere of peace and acceptance, which encourages them to freely express themselves without the fear of ridicule. Reiki encourages people to open up to their own truths, looking at the deeper issues that lie beneath their problem, and this helps when needing to source what the core issues are really about. I will always use Reiki as part of my Natural Therapies practice, as it brings peace and harmony into all aspects of my practice.

Becoming Energy Conscious

The concept of humans as energy meant absolutely nothing to me when I first learnt Reiki. But afterwards I remembered what I had been taught in science at high school. Everything in the universe was made up of atoms and these atoms were made up of smaller particles called protons, electrons and neutrons.

These resembled little electrical sparks or balls of light that attracted each other. Atoms vibrated and moved constantly which attracted other similar atoms, creating specific groups with similar combinations of moving protons, electrons and neutrons. These collective groups are what constitute all physical elements and substances known to man, including man himself.

We humans are made up of atoms and atoms are simply pure energy. I understood this to some extent but had no idea that I would have need of this information until much later in my life. Reiki helped to awaken the rest of my forgotten schoolbook science knowledge.

Changing Vibration

Have you ever wondered about objects that are made up of atoms but are really moving microscopic particles and not solid? How does something ever appear to be solid?

It was explained to me that it was a matter of density and vibration or speed of these moving atoms. As atoms attract atoms and gather together they become denser and appear to be solid. If they become slower and more static, they may vibrate such as wood.

Atoms that were less dense, which moved a little faster and less static, could be something like vegetation for example. Other atoms moving even faster would appear to be less dense such as water and eventually vapour or gases. The faster the atoms vibrated the less visible they become and the more moveable the energy form is.

An example I like to use often in my Reiki classes is that of water. Water atoms vibrate at the speed of liquid. However, if we add coldness we can freeze it and change its vibration to a solid, such as ice. Then if we boil the water with flame we can change it again back into liquid and then into steam, which vibrates as vapour.

While water, ice and steam can change their vibration they all still remain chemically H_2O – water. None of its original energy is ever lost; it is simply transformed into another vibration through the introduction of an intervening energy.

A molecule of water vibrating at a frequency of liquid experiences the world as water and is unable to relate to steam or ice, even though they are the same energy. It isn't until something changes the water that it is possible for it to experience the frequency of steam or ice.

This same concept can be applied to man's experience of his reality. There are at least as many realities as there are people, so an individual's life experience is his or her reality. It goes without saying that no two people experience the same thing the same way.

Everybody has their own thoughts and feelings and they are different to each other. Their experience of the world is unique because of this. It is a direct result of thoughts and feelings generated by their own vibrational energy's experience of reality.

The speed or vibration of moving energy particles is what determines its frequency, this frequency then determines the form in which the energy appears; either solid, liquids or gases, also animal, vegetable or mineral. These combinations of vibrational energy are what make up what we experience as our world.

This is why our world appears solid when, in fact, it is only energy vibrating together and dancing at many different frequencies. This energy dance is what we are experiencing as our environment and living three-dimensional reality.

Thoughts and feelings are only a higher form of the same energy, a higher vibration than physical energy but one that is constantly changing. This energy represents our awareness, allowing us a conscious experience of our world. Our conscious experience is relayed to us via our senses, which directly relates to our thoughts through our mind. This conscious experience is our life.

Your experience of this reality (your life) is determined also by your own vibrational energy (how fast you are vibrating.)

Since thought is a higher vibrational energy and is what enables us to experience life, then the higher one's thought vibration becomes, the more conscious experience of life one receives. Higher frequencies of energy must then represent higher consciousness, our awareness of life. If we are also made up of this same energy then man is a consciousness energy being.

The frequency of our personal awareness or consciousness will determine how broad our experience of life will be. This concept is relatively new to us on mass but is taught within some spiritual teachings. For me, it took learning Reiki as an energy science to put it in this context. Most people on the path to self-enlightenment need at some time to learn about the human energies of the body, the mind and its emotions, our feelings and soul, relating to the self.

It explains why some of us cannot relate to each other on some levels. We are all at different levels of awareness or energy and this creates a gap in our ability to understand or relate to each other.

I found many revelations as I came to understand how the human energy systems of mind, emotion, body and spirit worked.

There are many different energies in our universe. Reiki is just one of the many vibrations. Mankind is another and we are all reflections of the one Divine energy source.

The Energy Dance of Man

Man is a soul and rents a body with each incarnation; however, there is quite a lot of the human soul that cannot be seen in the physical form. The human body is a mass of energy and is divided up into two main parts. The first part is seen as the physical body, the second part is the aura or etheric energy body, which is a non-visible physical energy field. I liken our energy field to that of microwaves or radio or infrared waves, which are also not visible energy.

We have an emotional body and a mental body and extended out from that we have our spiritual body. This is the energy that we project to others through the extended body we call the etheric body or 'aura'.

All living things give off an electromagnetic field (aura) just like ours. The aura contains all our mental, emotional and spiritual body's information. I think of the aura as a kind of computer hard drive where we download information for storage. All these energy systems work together with the physical body relaying messages for it to be in balance and function properly. By only treating the physical body, if we are not well, we are not treating the whole person or the whole problem. The role of your energy system is to bring to your attention any imbalances, giving you an opportunity to treat them before they become a physical problem or illness.

Our aura is very sensitive and we pick up feelings or perceived inklings about others through the energy exchange when auras meet. If we are aware of this and become sensitive to it, we tend to get intuitional feelings about people's emotional states and their attitudes as a result. What we find is that quite often their conversation usually confirms what we already have perceived.

It's a sign that the intuitive side to our nature is developing and that we are becoming more sensitive to other people's energy vibrations that are picked up through our own aura. Many people become adept psychics when this sense is developed.

The aura is an electromagnetic field that surrounds the body about a metre or two in diameter and looks like an egg-shape. It is the soul's light force as it manifests through the body; the extended energy around the human body which alters in light and colour depending upon the state of physical, mental, emotional and spiritual health.

The aura is not usually seen by the naked eye, even though Kirlian photographers have documented its existence. It has various planes, each existing simultaneously within the auric field and inter-dimensionally overlaid within one another.

WE ARE ENERGY BEINGS!

Everything participates in a dance of energy. Our physical body is energy and continually changing. The cells in our physical body are renewed in less than two years. Imagine how many bodies you have already had. Our body utilises energy from five different sources – the sun, the earth's magnetic field, the food we eat and the water we drink, the air we breath, and the universal cosmic life-force where Reiki comes from. For example, we can't touch the sun, we can't smell it, we can't hear it or taste it, we can only see the light it produces and feel the warmth it gives. But we know that it makes us happy to see it, and plants need it to grow just as we do. It is part of our cosmos and it is a pure energy. Reiki is just like the sun. You can only feel its warmth and the sense of peace it gives you when you receive it. It, too, is part of our cosmos and is pure life-force energy, a love energy if you like, and we all know just how healing love can be. We cannot live without it.

Energies That Affect Us

Knowing now that we are made up of energy you can understand how, as people, we affect each other's energy. We all receive feelings about the people we meet and the places we visit.

Think about some of the places you visit that have a positive effect on you. Why is this? Now think about the places that have a negative effect on you. Why is this? You can apply these questions to people that you meet. Have you noticed how some people have a positive effect and others can have a negative effect. How do you like to be effected by the energy of another person or place?

You can see now why it is we are drawn to certain places and people. They usually have high vibrational energy, which makes us feel good as it increases our own energy by being around them. How we feel about people or places determines whether we return to them again or not. These feelings are felt because we are affected by the energy they give off. Everything has an energy vibration – people, places, businesses, houses, cars, animals, clothes and colours.

Question Time!

What colour do you associate **negative** energy with?..................

What colour do you associate **positive** energy with? ....

List things that drain your energy:..
List things that give you energy:..
How does **negative** energy affect you?..
How does **positive** energy affect you?...
List ways people can affect you **negatively**:..................................
List ways people can affect you **positively**:...................................
List **positive** emotions/thoughts:..
List **negative** emotions/thoughts:...

Which ones would you rather be feeling? I hope from this little exercise that you will see that positive energy gives you positive feelings and you think positive thoughts. While negative energy gives you negative feelings and negative thoughts.

Wouldn't it be true to say then that positive thoughts give positive energy, and negative thoughts give negative energy. Wouldn't you like to effect people in a positive way with your positive thoughts rather than a negative way with negative thoughts?

*Our thought, like plumbing,
need unblocking now and then.*

Just as you affect others with thought so you affect yourself with them. It is up to you how you choose to affect yourself with either negative or positive thinking. I know which ones I would choose, knowing now how they will effect my own energy level. Negative thoughts drain me, while positive thoughts empower me. Negative energy can attract negative energy, while positive energy attracts positive energy. When dealing with other people I have always treated them as I would wish to be treated. Even difficult people who sometimes exasperate us need positive energy to dissipate their own negative energy.

Remember back to a time when you were unhappy, maybe even a little depressed. How were your energy levels? I bet you felt drained and lethargic, not wanting to do anything. This is negative mental/emotional energy at work. It can be very draining. Now try to remember a happy time and think about your energy level then.

I'm sure that you were in high spirits and your energy was high also. This is positive mental/ emotional energy at work.

You may now understand how other people's mental and emotional energies can affect yours and why we get intuitional feelings about new prospective partners and friends fairly quickly. Realise now that you also affect people you meet in the very same way.

Deflect Negative Energy

When you feel intimidated or exasperated and frustrated by another person's mental or emotional energy, just send them a positive thought. It sounds too easy doesn't it? The best thoughts are of love, so send them unconditional love. Now I know this seems crazy but it works. If you send them positive thoughts, their higher selves will pick it up in the feeling of good vibes or energy. It automatically starts to deflect negative energy, as negative and positive cannot live in the same space. This confuses them because they feel their own negativity reflected back at them and they quite often stop. If they do not then it is not your fault. At least you know you have sent them good thoughts and tried to diffuse their negative energy with love.

Sending positive thoughts leaves their negative energy where it came from – with them. It has the affect of not allowing you to take it on board as yours. You can walk away from them feeling unaffected by them. I suggest that you try this exercise with the next person who affects you in this manner.

A great testing ground for this is in mid-flight during an argument or disagreement. Stop and remind yourself to come from love and see how it affects the argument. More than likely it will see it stop. Negative energy needs fuel to survive and it takes two or more to argue, so non-participation is still the best way to stop negativity from taking over. Nobody feels good when they argue. It is better to diffuse it and resolve the conflict with non-aggressive communication.

We all have a responsibility with how we affect each other's energy. No one wants to be around negative energy. Our emotional energy affects people every day and if for some reason you are with someone who is feeling a negative emotion then this can drain your energy without you even realising it.

As a hairdresser in my previous work, I saw and touched and talked with people all day long. No wonder I felt drained at the end of it. If you work with the public in any fashion, then chances are that they will affect your energy levels quite frequently without you realising it. This was one of the biggest reasons I learnt Reiki in the first place. Learning how to defuse negative energy helped me cope with negative clients, and it worked.

Reiki is positive loving universal life-force energy; it can only affect us in a positive manner. In Level 2 you can learn how to use Reiki energy to diffuse negative energy much quicker.

We literally feel how the other person reacts to us physically, emotionally, mentally and spiritually through the aura's ability to pick up energy vibrations. We tend to get perceived inklings as to how a person is feeling through our intuition. Although you may not be aware of this going on, your higher self and soul are.

I'll give you some examples of your aura at work.

1. Can you recall a person whom you felt was very angry, sick and upset when you met them (and this had nothing to do with you)? How did they affect you upon meeting them? Could you not sense that something was wrong. You may have begun feeling aggressive towards this person or felt that you should not have been there. You may have felt tension across the chest or feelings of anxiety.

2. Now, can you remember meeting someone who was happy and at peace within themselves. How did they affect you? Did they give you a sense of peace and calm? When you left them did you feel relaxed and good about yourself? This would have been felt through the sensitive energy exchanges within both your auras.

3. Have you ever met someone for the first time and just knew that you knew this person and as a result struck up an instant rapport? Conversely, have you met someone only to instantly dislike him or her for no apparent reason? What generally happens is that you are picking up on all their energy levels and don't feel comfortable with their energy. Sometimes this feeling comes about because they have a hidden mental or emotional agenda and you

are being warned about it through the aura's ability to sense or pick up on their projected mental/emotional energy.

Clever isn't it? However, we quite often dismiss our intuitive thoughts as being silly or selfish, not realising their true messages.

As you think so shall you be.

Our thoughts can transmit energy to others and also affect our own levels of physical energy. Telepathy is a very common feeling that can happen when we care about someone or work or live in a close environment.

ENERGY HEALING

By realising that human beings are made up of energy, one can comprehend new ways of looking at health and illness. In conjunction with medicinal drugs and surgical approaches, vibrational medicine like Reiki attempts to treat people with pure energy.

Central to the work of mental-spiritual integration, such as massage and Reili, is the concept that the physical body is the outward manifestation of thought patterns (many from childhood) of fears and traumas that we have allowed to penetrate our energy fields or auras.

Within specific locations of our aura we collect data through feelings, sensations, emotions, thoughts, memories and other non-physical experiences. These are what we report to our doctors and therapists in the form of physical ailments. Understanding how our physical symptoms are related to these locations within our aura will help us to understand the nature of different illnesses.

Healing with Reiki changes unhealthy conditions within the human energy system, promoting a healthy energy field/aura and producing harmony and balance. In this balanced state, humans become more conscious of 'self' and their connection to others and all living things. It helps us to be able to radiate positive energy from the chakras, our awareness is lifted and the healing process begins.

Layers of the Aura

The first layer – Primary health aura

This is the first part of the aura, the state between energy and matter composed of tiny energy lines and light beams generated by the living tissues of cells and the functions of human physiology. It emanates 2-5 centimetres from the body, as well as internally as the 'meridian grid system', used by acupuncturists, reflexologists and massage therapists.

The second layer – Emotional body

This portion of the aura is associated with feelings. All sensations, emotions and desires are part of this layer. Sometimes called the 'astral body', it holds all the memories and deep emotional responses to your experiences. Interaction of people takes place at this level.

You feel the difference, pleasant or unpleasant. People forming relationships form cords from their chakras connecting them. This layer is where we experience our relationships, abuse, job-related experiences and all traumas and joys. Its structure is quite fluid like clouds of fine substance in continual motion. The astral part of this layer is amorphous and is composed of clouds of colour. This extends 2-6 centimetres from the body.

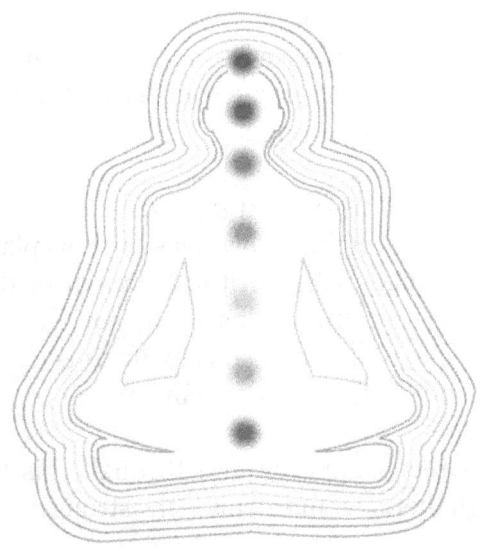

The third Layer – Mental body

A portion of the body comprising of thoughts, opinions, intellectual knowledge, memories, beliefs, and self-perceptions of identity and reality. It contains the structure of our ideas. Within this field thought forms can be seen. Clairvoyants connect at this level. It extends from 6-25 centimetres from the body. It is beyond the emotional body and is composed of a still finer substance.

The fourth Layer – Etheric body

This is energy webbing or the underlying foundation that holds together the aura as a holographic unit. This grid structure is what the physical body builds on. It carries the primal pattern of the individual's existence, and consciousness at all other levels of reality. It reflects all the possibility of the individual's current incarnation. It is at this level that sound transforms matter, which is most effective for healing the body. It extends 25-50 centimetres from the body.

The fifth Layer – Celestial body

This is the emotional level of the spiritual plane in which we experience spiritual ecstasy. Meditation, initiations such as Reiki attunements and transformational work is experienced on this level. It is the point of being where we begin to know that our connection is with the universe.

Through it we see light and love in everyone and everything. Some of our deepest emotional experiences are felt on this level. It extends 50-75 centimetres from the body.

The sixth Layer – The spiritual plane

This is the mental level of the individual's spiritual plane. It is where you connect knowingly with spirit and consist of the outer shell of the egg-shaped aura. It contains all the auric bodies associated with the present life the individual is living. It is composed of tiny threads of gold and silver (male and female essences) and holds the aura together.

All the chakras receive energy first through this level. Reiki is received through this layer first. This is the strongest, most resilient level of the auric field. Its power current pulses up and down the spine (the kundalini) carrying energies through the roots of each chakra, and connecting the energies taken through each chakra.

This plane holds the individual's present spiritual life's plan. It extends out roughly one metre from the body. Everything that happens to us during our life is registered by the spiritual body first. All past life memories are held within it.

THE CHAKRA SYSTEM

Discovery of the dormant wisdom hidden within our chakras leads to illumination through shifts in awareness, peace through serenity, health and well-being.

Knowledge of the *chakras* – and the techniques used to awaken them – was kept secret for centuries. But now, with increasing interest in Eastern philosophy and alternative medicine, the idea that there might be hidden energy forces within the human body is gathering acceptance in the West.

Although long thought of as being exclusive to the religions of India, the concept of these 'etheric' energy centres is not entirely alien to the West. Medieval alchemists had a similar system within the human body believed to correspond to, and could be influenced by, specific metals and plants.

The Judaic mystics describe a set of energy centres called sefirot and can be seen as the refined spiritual centres on the cabalistic Tree of Life, which can also be matched with points of the physical body. Buddhism, Sufism, Taoist Yoga and Tantric traditions all believe in degrees of this concept. In their individual practices, all these traditions encouraged gradual spiritual development with the belief that each chakra centre will open more as the initiate matures spiritually. Reiki, when used regularly, can help with these shifts of spiritual integration and evolvement.

The word chakra is a Sanskrit word meaning 'Wheel of Light' and is the unseen energy centre within the 'etheric' aura body. These centres ensure and stimulate health, vitality and, ultimately, enlightenment when activated.

Reiki helps to stimulate and balance these aspects through the chakras. Their spinning generates our electromagnetic field/aura.

This is the way the body receives energy and transmits energy to all other energy beings and to itself.

For every chakra there is a corresponding layer within the aura. Each chakra is associated with various kinds of evolution within our consciousness while taking care of physical organs and glands. Each has corresponding colours, stones, sounds, essential oils and crystals, which can help with its activation, stimulation and healing. These chakras are opened and activated only in accordance with an individual's level of awareness and understanding.

They can be a storehouse full of suppressed emotions and should not be unleashed without the guidance of a teacher or healer.

How do they work?

The chakras function as our energy lungs, or intake organs for energy from the universal life force, which then feeds our life or health field – our aura. The energy taken in through each chakra is sent to different parts of the body located in the area closest to it. This energy is very important for the healthy functioning of the auric field and affects us on all levels of the mind, emotions, body and spirit.

If a chakra stops functioning properly, becoming blocked, the intake of energy will be disturbed. This means that any physical parts served by that chakra will not get their needed energy supply. When any of the energy centres are blocked, the body will weaken as will its immune defences, and eventually disease will occur in that part of the body. But when each chakra is stimulated and energised, it spins faster, improving the physical, emotional, mental and spiritual functions with which it is associated.

During Reiki treatments we place our hands over these chakras to help them balance and begin to function better. A seasoned Reiki practitioner can scan the body with their hands and feel how the person's aura and chakras are doing before a treatment.

Using a dowsing crystal also helps us find out what is happening on an energy level within a particular chakra. Those who have the ability to see auras and chakras will know by the discolouration.

We have seven main chakras and some minor ones on joints and limbs. These chakras look like funnels and each funnel has its wider opening two to three centimetres from the outside of our body and is about 15 centimetres in diameter. The small tip of the chakra funnel connects to a tube or 'etheric' energy channel, which runs parallel to the spinal cord. It is through this tube that the energy channelled through all the chakras is released into our physical body, similar to electrical circuitry. The seven major chakras are located near the major nerve plexuses of the body.

Crown - Spiritual

3rd Eye - Perception

Throat - Expression

Heart - Love

Solar Plexus - Power

Sacral - Sex

Root - Survival

Chakra One – Base or Root of the Kundalini
This is located at the sacral-coccyx joint or perineum. It relates to our will to live and supplies the body with physical vitality. It supplies energy to the spinal column, the adrenal glands, and the kidneys.

This is where we integrate fear and the will to live. Governs the amount of life-force energy in an individual, and functions as action and the receiving of pleasure. Its element is Earth and vibrates as the colour RED.

If this chakra is blocked the person will not make a strong impression in the physical world. They will avoid physical activity, will be low in energy and may even be sickly. It leads to lacking of physical power.

All our basic instincts for survival are within the consciousness of this chakra. It deals with fight and flight.

Chakra Two – Sacral

The second chakra is located just above the pubic bone beneath the naval on the front and back of the body. It is the centre of the sacrum, which governs the emotional life of the individual. It is related to our sensuality and sexuality.

In women this centre is within the womb, and in men it is called the 'will' point and centred in the gonads. It governs the quantity of sexual energy. It sends energy to the immune system and helps us with our use of sex and food and is also known as our creative core centre. Its element is water and vibrates as the colour ORANGE.

If this chakra is blocked it leads to disappointing sexual potency. Little sexual drive, tending to avoid sex and dismissing it as a non-important pleasure, thus denying psychological nourishment of orgasm which bathes the body with life force. Issues of closeness through the sexual communion with another and self-imposed barriers are dealt with here. Deep-seated emotional behaviour can be dealt with through the consciousness of this chakra.

Chakra Three – Solar plexus

The third chakra is located in the solar plexus on the front and back of the body. It supplies the stomach and all related digestive organs such as liver, gall bladder, pancreas, spleen, and nervous system with energy. It is associated with our mind processes and is related to who we are in the universe and how we connect with others and take care of ourselves. It regulates our emotional life and human connectedness. We show sympathy/empathy, our desires and aspirations. Its element is fire and vibrates as the colour YELLOW.

If this centre is blocked we feel disconnected from the universe and feel lost, not belonging anywhere. Feelings become blocked and the ability to be able to feel sensations, emotions, energy, etc., is an issue within this chakra. One will not be aware of a deeper meaning to life and not be able to understand an individual's uniqueness within the universe. We become more apathetic towards our physical health. Developing a sense of how we feel in relation to and with others are all part of the consciousness of this chakra.

Chakra Four – Heart

The fourth chakra is in the middle of the chest and is the centre of spiritual awakening. Those who fully awaken the heart chakra have incredible experiences. It governs the ability for humans to give and receive love while learning about unconditional love. This is where we relate best to nature – our link with physical reality. It supplies energy to our heart, circulatory system, thymus, vagus nerve and upper back. Its element is air and vibrates as the colour GREEN.

If this centre is blocked there will be a lack of self love or an increase in selfishness. A person will have trouble loving, loving with a sense of giving without expecting anything in return. There will be an overwhelming sense of non-connectedness with all fellow humans and with all life. People try to own their mate or person they love. They will lack trust in their life and be quite fearful. Soul awareness of who we are as a soul and our role in the universe as an individual can be stimulated by the consciousness of this chakra.

Chakra Five – Throat

The fifth chakra is located in the front and back of the throat. It is associated with the senses of hearing, tasting and smelling. It supplies energy to the thyroid, the bronchi, lungs and alimentary canal. It is where mental creativity takes place with planning and scheming. It governs the power of speech and sound and the ability of the individual to express themselves. It is where we manifest and create on the physical plane. Vibrates as the colour BLUE.

When this centre is blocked we blame everything and everyone else for the wrongs in our life. There will be a lack of personal responsibility towards self and others. Our fears become manifested through negative thoughts and actions. Like attracts like.

There will be an inability to express thoughts, feelings and desires through speech, writing or sound (music). Trusting life is a big issue here.

Pride and a lack of self-esteem are affected and how one sees oneself in society. Fulfilment and success will be difficult to obtain. Bringing what you desire to have happen in your life is manifested into reality via this chakra.

Chakra Six – Third Eye or Brow

The sixth chakra is located in the middle of the forehead, both front and back of the head. Awakening this centre increases our psychic abilities and intuitive thoughts. It supplies energy to our pituitary gland, lower brain, left eye, nose, ears and nervous system. It is associated with our sense of sight and sense of time and space. It is directly related to our conceptual understanding and the carrying out of our ideas, step by step, to accomplish them. Vibrates as the colour VIOLET.

If this centre is blocked then a confused state of mind is common along with the inability to conceptualise ideas (create plans). Compulsive lying and even criminal activity is hatched from this centre. A lack of intuition and or spiritual integration within the person is usual. An inability to dream may occur also. This chakra develops all aspects of the mind's psyche. Stimulate the consciousness within this chakra and spiritual sight will develop.

Chakra Seven – Crown

The seventh chakra is located at the top of the head or crown, located around the pineal gland. It supplies energy to our upper brain and the right eye. It is associated with our experience of direct knowing and is related to the integration of personality with spirituality. This chakra regulates the amount of light an individual can photosynthesis; hence, it controls the amount of 'enlightenment' or 'consciousness' a person can accept. When fully activated it facilitates cosmic consciousness and total integration of mind, emotions, body and spirit. Vibrates to the entire colour spectrum, so it is WHITE.

If this centre is blocked then one probably does not have an experiential connection to spirituality or the concept of God. Because of this one would not understand what others are talking about when they speak of their spiritual experiences. Either a lack of faith would exist or a strong dogmatic belief would be a result also.

Energy Conscious

Once we become aware of how we affect each other and ourselves on an energy level, a shift occurs within our consciousness and we decide to take responsibility for our own energy. Maintaining our energy levels and staying in a positive mode will become important to us because of this new awareness.

Reiki not only brings about this energy consciousness it helps us to maintain our energy by staying more balanced as we observe our own behavior and attitudes. Observation of these aspects within oneself allows us to correct ourselves and shift any negativity that we may find. This is all part of taking control of your life. In reality we cannot change others, we can only change ourselves as this energy awareness lets us know who we are and how we affect others and take responsibility for this.

As we treat ourselves with Reiki the consciousness shifts that occur within each chakra sees us move on from many negative-learned mental and emotional behavioral responses. No longer is it necessary to spend years in therapy analyzing ourselves to infinity.

Reiki is an energy of love and love will always be the end result of using it. Whether it is used on others or ourselves, this energy helps to bring balance and awareness. It ultimately brings us back into wholeness, to beings of love and light, which is who we really are. If this it could happen on a global level, we would see an end to world wars and arguments or conflicts.

Reiki is helping to shift humanity's consciousness through awareness and healing of energy. Once we learn to take control of ourselves from this perspective we will improve our world's energy vibration, ultimately taking control of humanity's destiny into the Aquarian Age.

I believe that in the not to distant future this and many other teachings will become commonplace within our scholastic system. The need within people to discover and understand their personal energy system is rising like a giant wave.

The re-discovery of Reiki has come about as a direct result of mankind's group consciousness wanting to claim back this very natural information.

PART TWO

THE NEXT STEP

Deciding to learn Level Two Reiki is the next step. Like many things we learn throughout our life there is always a process that we must go through. Learning Reiki is no different. There is a process to it and this takes its own time. For each of us as individuals this time factor varies in duration depending on the amount of Reiki treatments one gives oneself initially, and one's enthusiasm to learn more about self and the metaphysics of the Reiki energy. It's the regular use of the Reiki that brings about its awareness, not just the attunements received during a Level One seminar. Because of this it is not feasible for Reiki to be understood or integrated in just one weekend workshop. I find it harder to write about something that needs to be experienced firsthand in order for it to be understood at all.

Most Reiki Masters usually suggest that there be a minimum of at least one to two months before progressing from Level One to Level Two. This is simply because it takes time to completely understand and absorb the changes that can be created by the four attunements given during the first level. The entire human physiological and subtle body energies undergo alteration of their bio-magnetic energy, so there can be delayed healing and reactions to this subtle healing.

For some students the receiving of Reiki energy through the attunement process brings about massive changes, or shifts, as we often call them. This is all part of the healing process that takes place and is due to the emotional, physical and mental status of the student's psyche at the time of the attunements. This is determined by any unresolved issues or physical imbalances pre-existing the four attunements given in Level One.

The first 21 days after these first four attunements is usually dynamic for all students. I always encourage students to have at least completed their 21-day cleansing period before they consider doing the next level. Sufficient time between first and second degree Reiki prepares the student for the next quantum leap into the higher levels of consciousness that Second Level Reiki energy attunements help to bring about.

As you begin your journey into this new and exciting vibration, let go of any thoughts that the next level will be just more of the same energy.

What You Will Experience

Being initiated into Level Two is a major step and commitment to furthering the development of one's mind, body and spirit through the using of Reiki energy. We find for many students that on completion of the Second Level a whole new world of people in need of natural healing will be presented to them. There is an expansion that takes place within the consciousness of all Second Level students. Again this takes time to integrate and is different for every individual.

The frequency of our individual personal consciousness determines how broad our life experience will be. In other words, as we lift our energy with the use of Reiki and expand our own energy vibration our consciousness will grow, allowing us a better experience of our reality – life. The energy itself creates an expanded awareness and in this way can be used for personal transformation, clarity, healing and releasing, etc.

The intent of further study with Second Level is to expand our conscious understanding of the uses of Reiki, plus establish a spiritual integrity, and more in-depth mental and emotional healing process usually begins. We now wish to establish professionalism in our practice of Reiki.

Level Two energy usually helps with more of our journey within, helping to discover the spiritual soul self. I have found that each soul's purpose begins presenting itself, becoming more important to students as they learn to listen to their own intuition. Level Two energy embodies an impulse towards more self-realisation and indicates a path that we must follow, not from our ego ulterior motives but from the core of our own individuality or soul.

As we work with this level of energy we learn to trust ourselves, allowing growth and change to take place in all areas of our lives. As a natural progression we experience an expanded consciousness helping us to be ready to accept anything now and at any time. We begin to see a deeper pattern to our life.

While students work with the energy of Level Two on themselves they become more sensitive to the energies of all levels of mind, body and spirit within self and others. It is a natural progression to pick up on the emotions of others and the frustrations or mental blocks within their mind, body or spirit. Many can feel the pain of others and must learn not to take it on board as their own. Spiritual connections become increasingly important after Level Two as each individual soul seeks out like-minded energy for purposeful connections.

Level Two sees many students begin to develop telepathy, aura vision, clairvoyance or clairaudience skills as a direct result of their awareness of being stimulated by the attunements. However, each of us must develop these skills at our own speed. The more we use the energy on ourselves the faster we progress. Some will begin to question many aspects of their life, discovering it is no longer enough that they accept what society's responses and rules dictate. Most begin their own journey on a quest for inner truth. Experiencing Level Two energy provides us with an opportunity to evaluate our spiritual integrity by exercising our free will through choice creating change, helping us to obtain spiritual integration in everyday life.

> *If one desires a change,*
> *one must be that change*
> *before that change*
> *can take place.*
>
> *- Gita Bellini*

DIFFERENT VIBRATIONAL ENERGY

Second Level Reiki energy is an entirely different vibrational energy to the First Level. Level One is warm and gentle and radiates out of the entire hand. Second Level sends an intense beam of energy shooting from the palm chakra. Because of this it can be used for beaming across rooms and for scanning the aura. Hand sensations become an important part of the understanding of energy at this level. We have found that the hands and arms will also go through an adjustment period as the channels, through which the Reiki energy flows, open more fully.

The energy begins to flow out of your hands more, and possible much faster. There is a need now to pay more attention to the variance of temperature each hand will experience. The palm and the back of the hand will quite often send different messages to the brain.

There can be a difference between what you feel and what your client feels. You may have the feeling of coolness in your hands while the client experiences heat. The cooling effect is usually because you are sending massive amounts of energy. This can be experienced in reverse where the hand is cool to the client and hot to you. The imbalanced energy is being transferred out or extracted from the client through your hands out through your aura's energy. Don't worry, this energy will not be absorbed by you, it simply passes through.

Hand Sensations

As you have begun to use Reiki you may have noticed some tingling or strange sensations going on in you hands. Both practitioner and client most frequently experience heat.

However, a practitioner may also feel tingling, cold, pulsations, and some aches or pain to various degrees. Do not be alarmed at this, it is all quite normal. With practical experience you will come to understand what these all mean to you and will decide how best to act upon this added information for the well-being of your client. So be aware of your hands and body at all times during treatments.

Understanding the association of these areas on our hands to the body assists in feeling where problems are manifesting within your client.

This is in no way a diagnosis. It merely indicates to the practitioner that a little more energy is required in that area, and possibly other Reiki treatments will be required.

I have found that three consecutive treatments, initially, usually sees a remarked difference in my clients' well-being.

1. Crown
2. Pineal
3. Pituitary
4. Eyes
5. Sinus
6. Mouth
7. Ears
8. Throat
9. Occipital bone
10. Upper spine... back of neck

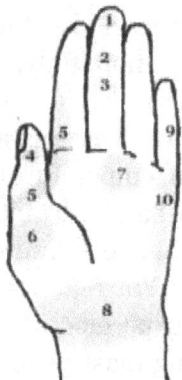

The universal life force of Reiki has innate intelligence and gives or takes energy according to the person's need to re-establish balance within the body's energy system. Because of this mechanism there is no possibility of overdosing on Reiki energy. Persons receiving Reiki only take what is needed at that time for their highest good.

REIKI TWO SYMBOLOGY

In Dianne Steins' popular book, *Essential Reiki*, symbols are covered quite extensively and I feel no need to follow suit. Instead, I prefer to deal with the processes and the consciousness shifts that these energy symbols help to bring about.

Each symbol has a different application, unlocking different aspects of the self, all stemming from the one source – Reiki. These are three most widely used Level Two symbols taught in most Reiki two seminars around the world today.

The Cho-ku-rei's Consciousness

The first symbol is called the *Cho-ku-rei*. It is an empowerment symbol and helps to operate the other symbols. In this manner it is the key to the Reiki energy and the forerunner to enable change. I teach this during Level One, however, it is generally taught in Level Two seminars. This symbol helps to turn on other Level Two symbols, bringing in Second Level energy. It is independent by nature and works well on its own and can be placed over all the chakras and anywhere else you wish to use it.

You cannot overuse this symbol or overdose on Reiki because when the cup is full it can take in no more.

Its consciousness helps to prepare us on sub-conscious levels for change. It allows the energy shifts that are required to take place, helping our acceptance of the changes. It is generally used over most areas when healing, and amplifies the energy when needed. Used with the *Sei-hei-ki* and the *Divinity* it assists us with releasing trapped feelings by unseen energy blockages that would otherwise hinder our natural growth.

The Sei-hei-ki's Consciousness

The next symbol is the *Sei-hei-ki*. This helps to heal the deeper mental emotional states within our subconscious mind. This symbol is always used in conjunction with the *Chokurei* as it needs its energy to operate it fully.

The application of this symbol is very important for healing the emotional body. Its energy has the ability to bring up from deep within our subconscious any emotional issues that we need to let go of, which will bring us back into balance. Any negative belief patterns that do not serve our highest good are presented to us in a fashion that allows us to gently move through them, helping us to deal with our fears or emotions related to these patterns. In this way the *Sei-hei-ki* offers us the opportunity for powerful inner healing, transforming our lower nature (negative thoughts and feelings)

with the help of our higher self through the use of Reiki. We call this transmutation.

This is part of the process of Reiki that has to be felt to be understood. Many Reiki practitioners do not fully understand that this is all part of what the energy of Reiki can help to bring about. This is why Reiki is a personal self-transformational tool as well as being an energy healing modality. It heals the inner self from the core of our being to the physical body. It helps us to look at patterns of beliefs that do not serve our purpose.

The *Sei-hei-ki* allows us to travel through the corridors of our mind helping us look at the darker side (negative aspects) of our nature. Through this self-observation we are able to see areas that may need adjustment or improvement within our behaviour patterns and emotional reactions. This kind of self-observation offers us the opportunity to correct any aspects of ourselves that we do not like and would rather change. It has the ability to speed up our processes of discernment in relation to creating changes in our life.

What I have discovered with my own observation of self and clients is that Level Two energy enables this to transpire with more ease than if the energy were not used. It takes the human conscious mind much longer to work through difficult patches of adjustment in our lives without the use of Reiki.

I see Second Level Reiki as the lifesaver of human nature during crisis. Many of those who tend to move onto this level are either at the crossroads within their life or at a crisis point wanting radical change. Needing to move through and change their mental and emotional patterns of behaviour, they seek Reiki as a tool for assistance.

As a result they are able to assist their own inner healing process through self-treatments. Many tears are shed during this time, a great relief is felt as they gently learn to unburden themselves in privacy, healing their own hurts without the need for years of therapy and counselling. This symbol is revolutionising our ability to see ourselves with more clarity and take back our dignity and control from within. It opens the doors to the god source from within. It helps many look deeply at and accept Christ consciousness as a part of accepting real unconditional love of oneself. These attributes see profound inner changes take place that affect a person's life spiritually.

This symbols embodies the impulses towards forgiveness of those in our life who we feel may have wronged us. This forgiveness then extends to oneself and accepts our part played in the sea of dramas that have unfolded for us. One of the best means of letting go is to learn to forgive the people and circumstances that were involved with any hurtful experiences. Blaming others for our hurt feelings seems easier at the time. We need to learn to forgive their lack of love and understanding or fears that their pain created which they inadvertently projected onto us. When we can let go of pain and suffering and forgive, we forgive ourselves as well.

Forgiveness is next to Godliness and speeds up the healing process. Often we feel life has been unfair and we hold onto the notion of this for far too long. Loss of love on any level feels unfair as does feelings of persecution. Forgiveness, if it is not allowed, turns to bitterness and resentment and makes for unpleasant illnesses later in life if it goes unchecked.

Symbol Politics

There has been much ado about Reiki symbols. It must first be understood that the physical aspects of symbology (either drawing them or visualising them) is inferior to the energy that they are able to help generate. It has always been the motive or mental and emotional intent upon the use of a symbol that gives that symbol an energy consciousness, not the symbol itself. Having said this, we can see why there are so many versions of similar symbols all representing the same or similar interpreted consciousness. This lack of understanding has seen many teaching masters come undone as they denigrate other Reiki practitioners who are using different symbology.

It is well known that Hawaya Takata, who brought Reiki to the West in about 1970, taught most of her 22 Masters a little differently, allowing for their own individual inner guidance to have its rite of passage. She saw no harm in the interpretation on a physical level being a little dissimilar. It was always the spiritual intent aligned with Divine purpose that mattered most within the Master.

When I first learnt the Reiki symbols in Level Two, I was taught to do them specifically one way and told that it was most important to learn them properly or they would not work. I was also told never to show or discuss them with anyone else as they may be misused. I realised later, of course, that this is not necessarily true and found this kind of teaching to be fear based. Secrecy breeds fear and lacks integrity or trust. Many have taken sacredness to mean secrecy – this is not so. Life itself is sacred; it is only the fearful mind that needs secrecy to guard information. Secrecy has never stopped wars in the past or human nature from exploring its potential in any direction. Even if others have tried to misuse Reiki symbols, they cannot be abused or misused. A group consciousness and a divine law govern them. There are no secrets in the universe.

The specific use of symbols simply trains the mind of the Reiki practitioner to align their mental and emotional intent with the heart, focusing on the purpose of healing with the particular symbol's energy.

Reiki symbols have an important role. They bring together a specific energy focus; we become co-creators to manifest energy when we use them. As Reiki practitioners we are attuned to a specific set of symbols, which increases their influence on us. Each time you actively use these healing symbols, you connect to their consciousness and amplify its meaning and energy. The first symbols taught in Level One have a subtle energy, however, when using Level Two energy they become amplified and more effective in their specific use and application.

THE HON-SHA-ZE-SHO-NEN

The third symbol taught in Level Two is the *Hon-sha-ze-sho-nen*, known as the cosmic telephone and used mainly for distance healing. This symbol takes people into their third eye's ability to transcend time and space, thus developing any psychic gifts that maybe lying dormant below the surface of an intuitive personality. While not everyone is aware of this, it happens slowly and only at the pace of a person's developing consciousness. Nothing ever happens to us unless we are ready for it.

This symbol helps most Reiki practitioners move into a more metaphysical awareness of life as we know it. It helps them move into the realm of spirit guides and angelic healers, slowly opening the doors to cosmic consciousness. It has the ability to help heal karma and remaining issues from past lives if used as a healing symbol.

It connects the healee with the healer on a spirit-to-spirit basis. While connected, the healer may feel pain, emotions, thoughts or sensations concerning the healee on a psychic level. It takes a while to become proficient with this kind of healing and guidance is a must. Contact with your teaching master is advised while you are learning how best to use this healing.

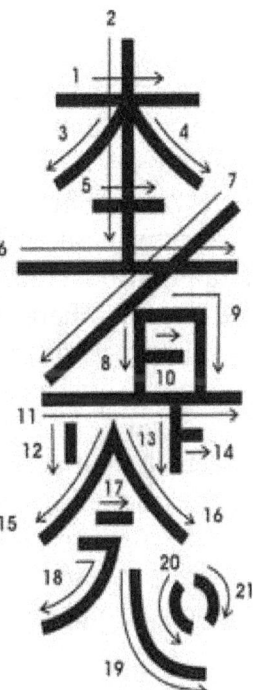

SENDING ENERGY

I like to teach beaming techniques for sending the Reiki energy to project energy across a room for the purpose of healing or assisting another person's energy. Scanning the aura before healing and learning to use the hands as energy detectors helps students to become more sensitised to feeling the energy of the aura. It is a learned skill and takes practice.

Man has been able to send much energy through time and space, such as radio waves, television pictures and electronic digital phones. We are unable to see these forms of transmission as they are sent through our atmosphere. Even though we cannot see them we accept that they exist because we either see a picture or get a sound. We cannot see Reiki either but we know it exists because we feel its warmth and sense of peace and well-being.

Those who have experienced receiving a distance healing can feel it and remark on its effects of calmness and warmth. Healing at a distance is the act of making contact with a person who is not in your physical presence. There are no rigid rules, do's or don'ts in distance healing. During a seminar any technique taught is simply a guideline. Ultimately, students are encouraged to practice and discover the way that suits them best. Most people begin to use this technique for healing family and friends in other parts of the country and the world.

This technique is quite simple and I was surprised at its effectiveness when I first learnt it. Distance healing has many applications. Many Reiki channels send to troubled spots on our globe (and there are plenty of those to choose from at the moment). This is just one of the ways you could use this technique if you wish to be of service to humanity.

Sending to a friend in hospital, having a baby or an operation or dentist treatment, or going for an interview is another. Some Reiki practitioners check newspapers for disasters or accidents and send to the people involved. Others use grids and crystals to send energy across and around the earth. The uses and applications for the Reiki energy from this standpoint are limitless.

Sending to the Past

As Reiki is a spiritual energy it has the ability to transcend time and space and can be sent to treat the past. This can be very effective in clearing mental negative belief patterns from childhood or emotional debris from your past by balancing it in the now, enabling you to let go and heal those hurts from the past. The manner in which you learn this is taught at a Second Level workshop. We also teach how to do a Reiki rebirth, treating your whole life from conception to present day.

Absent healing is governed by a Divine law – *thy will be done not mine* – and cannot be abused in any way. A person's higher self must be asked first for permission to qualify and accept the Reiki energy being sent. It doesn't matter whether the individual has verbally asked for the absent healing. It depends on his or her subconscious intent to qualify for the unconditional love sent for their personal healing. If the healee's higher self does not wish to accept the healing, the energy will not flow from the hands of the person sending.

The distance healing symbols may vary within different teachings of Reiki, and it does not matter. I liken the *Hon-sha-ze-sho-nen* to a cosmic telephone connecting you in a celestial way to another person's energy from a distance, *spirit to spirit*.

For many years the church has utilised such things as prayer to help people who were ill in some way, tapping into group Christ consciousness and love for the purpose of healing. This is a kind of absent healing and has been used for thousands of years. The Tibetan Buddhist monks have also been sending energy for healing for thousands of years through the use of symbology. The difference with prayer and Reiki is the specific use of symbols to bring through and send the vibrational healing energy we call Reiki.

The Procedure for Sending

From the many teachings available I have found that there are a few ways to send Reiki healing energy. Before you start you may want to find something that reminds you of the person, such as a photo, a pendant or ring they gave you, or some such item. If you have nothing of this nature, do not worry it, is enough to write their name and address on a piece of paper.

Visualise the person and imagine that you are there in person doing the healing session. Any of these methods will help you to connect with their energy.

1. Take the photo or paper with their name and address, etc, and hold it between your hands about 10 cm apart.

2. Do your invocation or prayer and ask their higher self for permission, then visualise the three symbols on the healee's third eye in sequence, wait for the energy to fill you hands. It will feel like an invisible cushion or sponge between your hands. Your hands will turn on.

3. Once connected you may begin to direct the healing session. Don't forget to use your symbols just as you would in a normal healing session.

One way is to visualise yourself doing the healing in person. You could use a medium such as a cushion or teddy bear as a structure to activate or send the energy, using different parts to represent front, back, head, legs and so on.

Some people imagine the person as very small and hold them cupped between their hands to carry out the healing. Another method is to use you own body, such as the left knee, then left thigh, then right knee, then right thigh. It does not matter how you do it as long as you can feel the energy; then send in four lots of five minutes.

Using your body, cushion or proxy to send

The first five minutes is for the head positions.

My right knee/corner of this cushion now corresponds to the four head positions of (name of healee).

The second five minutes is for the front positions.

My right thigh/corner of this cushion now corresponds to the four front positions of............

The third five minutes is for the back positions.

My left knee/corner of this cushion now corresponds to the five back positions of...........

The last five minutes is for the leg positions.

My left thigh/corner of this cushion now corresponds to the leg positions of ....

Five minutes sent this way is equivalent to about 20 minutes normally. So a 20-minute session is roughly the same as full treatment. Be aware of your hands as they draw the energy.

Closing the Distance Treatment

Bring your hands, 10 cm apart, back up in front of you. Visualise Buddha getting smaller and smaller between your hands and ask to close and release from the receiver's energy. You may like to say, *the Buddha in me says goodbye to the Buddha in you*. You will feel your hands being drawn together. By the time your fingertips meet the energy connection has disconnected. When a healing is done return to the present and forget about it. You must release and then ground yourself properly immediately after. Always end by sending the individual back into the care of the Divine creator.

By using the *Hon-sha-ze-sho-nen* you can direct or program the distance healing to be repeated more than once. You can also tell it to repeat at designated times, but put a limit on it depending on the required healing. You may designate that the healing repeat for as long as the person requires, or at a specific time of day.

When you begin to send distance healing, do one person at a time. After you have used the techniques and feel confident then you may wish to send to more than one person at a time. Simultaneous transmissions will not give you the same awareness of the people to whom the energy is sent as one to one does. I advise establishing one on one first in the initial three treatments before you add them to a group.

Some like to program crystal grids and pyramids to send to specific people at specific times. They do this by meditating, using the Reiki symbols and sending energy to the crystal. Crystals are transformers or transducers of energy and can be used in many fashions for healing.

Build up gradually and gain knowledge and expertise as you practice. In this way your healing ability will grow along with your confidence.

There are no limits
when it comes to loving and caring.
For if we limit our love,
we block its natural flow.

THE DOORS OF PERCEPTION

There are mainly two aspects that help us directly relate to our spiritual nature. When stimulated they open the doors to our inner perception allowing us to move through different kinds of spiritual awakenings. One of these doors lies deep within our heart; the other lies deep within our mind.

As we open either of these doors it allows for more awareness to penetrate our consciousness. We experience shifts in what we perceived as our reality. The more open we become the more life experiences we will avail ourselves of. These experiences, whether they are love or understanding, help to shift our original limited perceptions based on past limited experiences.

Man's basic difference from animals is simply that he uses his mind to communicate with spoken words and language in a way that animals are unable. Animals think in two dimensions, using only their more basic instincts, whereas humans think in three and often four dimensions. We are able to store and access a great deal of information of all kinds within our mind's memory. The mental energy that we generate and use to communicate with is what makes us a higher energy vibrational expression than that of animals. Humans are considered to be king of the animal kingdom only because we have this higher vibration of mental energy and the ability to communicate and express ourselves in ways that they cant. It has given us the ability to consciously explore ourselves more on the mental/emotional and spiritual planes.

Like animals we use to have stronger peripheral vision, our sense of smell was much keener and we could hear messages on the winds from great distances and through the ground of Mother

Earth. We have lost most of the ability to use our more instinctual nature. It has been educated out of our memory over eons of time and resurfaced in our ability to be more intuitive. We became more aware of the seasons and how this affected us as beings. We once relied on our intuition and not the more persistent intellectual voices of doubt and reason that we listen to now. This, of course, is not new knowledge to us; however, it has its place when looking at man's ability to perceive his reality.

When we look closer at man's evolving shifts in perception, it helps us understand the changing tides of consciousness. When I speak of consciousness I am talking about the mind's perception or awareness at that time of what it sees as being its reality. This helps us now understand better the different consciousness levels that we travel through during personal healing, spiritual awareness and higher consciousness.

The Heart and Mind

Love is the universal energy that binds all dimensions and realities. It is the energy consciousness of the heart and has been known to move mountains. It is my belief that there is nothing that love cannot achieve when linked with positive mental energy. It is through evoking the love energy that we are able to consciously experience the divine or God source.

This connection can be made in many ways of which Reiki is just one. Mental energy, when focused with loving divine intent, can achieve great results, especially when healing. However, many simply try to use the mind as a tool for reaching spiritual heights with meditation. Meditation is simply a way of learning to hone, tame and focus the mind. It can be during focused meditation that the purity of intention surfaces, which sees us move into right action and right speech.

When the mental focus is aligned with the heart's desires then anything is possible. The energy generated can then be used for any number of things, one of which is healing. Reiki helps many reach the energy of love via the heart chakra. However, the energy of Reiki can also help us to hone and focus the mind enabling us to better direct that love energy at will. I have found that most people, while experiencing Reiki, feel a shift take place within their awareness at the time they have hands on. Many use the energy of Reiki for just this purpose.

It helps them to focus and meditate simply because they relax on all levels and so are able to reach new altered states of awareness. It is during these altered states that we are able to get more clarity about problems and work through deeper issues of a mental and emotional nature.

Reiki is one of the best tools I know for focusing the mind and our emotions, taking them both under control through contemplation during meditation. Then whilst meditating we are able to deal with the issues, correcting our thoughts that cloud our conscious mental judgments by using our higher-mind's energy (or super conscious) coupled with divine love. This takes us from the mundane plane to the spiritual realms and allows for transmutation of thoughts, attitudes, feelings, emotions, behaviour and illness from the lower ego plane of separation to the higher soul plane of unconditional love and unity.

MEDITATION AS A TOOL

Mystics and magicians have used meditation techniques in the West for centuries, but only in the second half of the 20th century have they become a part of what many now term the 'New Age Consciousness'.

In the West it is generally believed that knowledge can only be attained through the mind via study and that wisdom comes mainly through experience. We pride ourselves on being realistic and practical, dismissing the idea that sitting in quiet contemplation can be anything more than rest and recuperation. And yet all of us inevitably meditate to some degree everyday of our lives – and are better for it. Whenever we lose ourselves in daydreaming or an activity that requires total concentration to the exclusion of everything else, we are actually engaging in a form of meditation. But the pleasure we get from these moments is usually fleeting and is soon dispelled by the invasion of conflicting thoughts, regrets and anxieties with which we usually absorb and indulge ourselves.

The great sages and spiritual teachers of the world have all suggested that if we can still our minds for even 10 minutes each day by concentrating on something simple such as a candle flame, it is possible to obtain the peace of mind which normally eludes us, causing much frustration and ill-health.

The secret of meditation is stillness, it allows the focusing of mental and spiritual energy.

People in the West have often confused relaxation with recreation. While obviously idle pursuits such as watching television and reading might focus the mind's attention, they do not still the mind. In order for us to gain access to the doors of cosmic consciousness and shift perception to the supreme wisdom, which is locked deep within our subconscious, we must first learn to still our restless minds.

The mind may be in perpetual motion but it rarely moves in one direction for very long. It tends to dart all over the place. This wastes our greatest resource – mental energy – causing most of us to seek stimulation rather than stillness. Meditation focuses these scattered pinpoints of light that are our thoughts like a laser beam.

Focusing on a point in the mind's eye, or on a candle flame, or the breath, reduces mental activity and allows the practitioner of meditation to contact the higher self, which has all the answers we seek. But, like everything else, this process takes time, discipline, patience and practice. The mind must be retuned to a higher frequency if it is to receive true wisdom from the depths within.

Meditation is a time when you discover that you are the architect of your mind.

Through meditation the ego, which creates the illusions of fear and separation, is slowly subdued. The meditator then becomes one with the object of his or her meditation, sometimes just for an instant, ultimately for eternity. Spiritual practices use meditation for purifying the mind and taking control of the emotions. Affirmations of divine love, compassion, happiness and joyfulness can be used to focus our energy within the mind during meditations.

It is these kinds of spiritual discipline that can help those seeking to raise their vibrations to evolve to much greater heights of spiritual evolvement. Regular meditation of this nature can improve clarity of thought; help concentration and health, as well as giving peace of mind, a calmer disposition and generally a more positive attitude towards others and to life.

Although the practice of meditation is very often solitary, extraordinary effects have been claimed for group meditations. For these reasons we use meditation to help relax and expand the mind, helping it focus during the course of learning Reiki.

Meditation before an attunement also helps elevate the students' mental awareness so that they may have a more conscious experience of their attunement process. In this way new students begin to understand that there is a direct relationship between their mind and their energy.

Basic Principals of Meditation

1. Try to establish the habit of meditation. Condition yourself by meditating at the same time each day and it will gradually become easier to settle into it. The ego is easily trained through routine and self-discipline.
2. Choose a place where you will not be disturbed and disconnect the phone. You may like to use a Walkman and listen to a favourite meditation tape or relaxing music.
3. Sit in a comfortable chair or in the lotus position or half lotus position with your back, neck and head in a straight and upright position. Try to discipline yourself to sit in a certain posture as this aids in training the mind and body to respond to the discipline. However, comfort is important.
4. Try not to let external thoughts distract you. Count your breaths in cycles of 3 to 5 if it helps to focus your attention while you relax into your meditation. If thoughts come into your mind, observe them with indifference, and then let them pass. Eventually, you won't need to do this.

5. Choose your focus for each meditation before you begin. It may be an affirmation of love or a mantra. It could be objects in front of you such as a burning candle; or imagine a white dot, a simple shape or symbol, number or colour. Later, these can be developed into visualisations to create the habit of positive thoughts to activate the chakras and heal the body.
6. Don't try too hard. Above all, relax and don't worry. It gets easier with practice.

Our Mental Processes

To become better architects of the mind we must first learn the mechanics of thinking and how our thought processes work.

In understanding the basics of the mind and how it works we can begin to understand that it only believes what we tell it. Our mind is our main central computer and collects all data throughout our life, on all levels of mind, body, emotions and spirit. In other words, it is your control panel and you drive the vehicle – your body – with your mind. What we begin to recognise is the fact that we are in control of ourselves as a physical vehicle. Or are we? It is through the mind that we experience our thoughts, emotions, reactions, behaviour patterns, health, feelings, dreams, fears, memory and intellect. Nothing ever *just* happens in our life. We have to have thoughts first. Our thoughts run our life and this is reflected in our life as reality. We co-create our life through our thinking. As we think so we are.

Our thoughts are the ancestors of our actions.

We all have a personality, and this is the person we reflect to others as being who we really are. We show and identify our personality externally with our attitudes and reflected beliefs, by the colours and style of our clothes and hair, by the way we conduct ourselves when in public, by how we treat others, by how we earn our living, by the house we live in and the car that we drive. These are the things that people see and use to perceive and make judgments of who we are.

Wrong or right, this has been the process in the past by which we try to understand who a person is. It falls short however, as it only gives us part of a visual picture of what is happening in their life at the present moment. We all know that things change in our life so often that it doesn't tell us who they really are at all. It isn't until we talk to someone that we begin to gain insight as to who they are really on the inside.

This concept, when applied to the self, is the same. When we learn to talk to ourselves and relate to our thoughts and feelings then we can begin to understand our true nature. Our inner spirit will communicate to us through our intuitive mind if we allow it.

The Levels of Our Mind

Many seekers of spiritual enlightenment do not yet understand the evolvement processes that go on within the workings of their own mind. To be able to access or get to higher levels of consciousness it helps if we learn to interpret the three main levels of our mind. They are the *Conscious Mind*, the *Subconscious Mind* and the *Superconscious Mind* or higher self.

Each functions on a different energy vibrational frequency, giving us different depths of insight into our own nature and life as we know it. We have the capacity to access any level and the information within at will during the course of thinking.

Of course, we do not usually consciously think, 'now which part of my mind had that thought?' Usually, it all happens without us realising it.

The Conscious Mind

This is that part of us that deals with everyday physical things and draws on its information through the main functions of our body's senses. All our basic survival needs are transmitted to the conscious mind and we act according to these needs. The conscious mind helps us to adapt to the physical plane and our immediate surroundings and environment. It deals predominately with sensations, which it gathers from our senses of sight, taste, touch, smell and hearing.

The conscious mind tells us when we are warm, cold, wet or dry, hungry or tired and what we need to do next. The conscious mind

The Seven Planes of Reality

Plane	Name	Description	Reiki / Consciousness
DIVINE PLANE	**Goddess/God**	Creation; Deity; Oneness; Nirvana/Bliss.	Cosmic Planetry Consciousness
SOUL PLANE	**Angelic Realms**	Spark of Oneness within us all; enlightenment; human divinity; directed spiritual will; divinity in manifestation; directs soul to evolution and enlightenment.	**Reiki Master** — Human Enlightenment
SPIRITUAL PLANE	**Christ**	Alchemical marriage or union; altruistic acts; soul-directed life; unconditional love; wisdom; permanent polorisation to indwelling spiritual self.	**Reiki Level Two** — Human Spiritual Awareness & Higher Consciousness
INTUITIONAL PLANE	**Buddhas**	Transpersonal; love; psychic abilities; telepathy; clairvoyance; imagination; collective higher states of consciousness.	
MENTAL PLANE	**Avatars/Adepts**	Consciousness; fantasy; dreams; memory-information storage; current information gathering; brain functions (ego, thinking); brain-body interaction.	
EMOTIONAL PLANE	**Human Icons**	Love; compassion; complex emotions; feeling; sympathy; empathy; primal emotions; anger; fear; pleasure.	**Reiki Level One** — Human Personality
PHYSICAL PLANE	**Nature**	Electricity; magnetic; air; fire; water; earth; smell; taste; touch; sight; light; sound; bodily functions.	

deals with our basic intellect and the body's desire for food, sex and stimulation of all the senses. The conscious mind is always busy dealing with the physical attributes of our daily life's routines and experiences. It is thinking about what it is doing in the now and making plans about the day-to-day business and social activities. *Beta* is the name given to the brainwaves of the conscious mind.

THE SUBCONSCIOUS MIND

This is completely different by nature than the conscious mind. It draws information from additional sources – that of our emotions and beliefs. It relies on our thoughts and feelings to tell us what to store as information in our memory bank. These feelings or emotions are usually gathered by way of our physical experiences felt originally from the conscious mind.

Places, situations, people, food, sexual experience, touch or circumstance is recorded in a long-term emotional memory file for future reference. Our feelings thoughts and emotions are governed by our *reactions* to all external stimulation.

The subconscious mind helps with the development and expression of our emotions. How we are effected by and feel about what we see, taste, touch, smell or hear is recorded. It records our mental and emotional reactions to everything that happens to us during our lifetime, negative or positive. It has the amazing capacity to memorise all our experiences, good bad or otherwise.

The subconscious also helps us to express ourselves with our mental processing of information, the forming of thoughts, ideas and communication. It also helps us to solidify our understanding of our mental reality our personal identity or personality. Much of this information is gathered over a long period of time, helping us to form personal belief patterns which also determine our personal behavioural patterns. We form attitudes at this level based on certain conditions of upbringing, race, colour, religious beliefs, culture at birth, country of birth, parents, friends, schooling and education, chosen profession, related job experiences, and the relationships we have with others all play their part. We usually relate all of this through our conversations with others. The subconscious mind is always reacting and processing our feelings and thoughts. When we look into the subconscious mind we are able to see who we have become as a result of our experiences and the way they affected us. *Alpha* is the name given to the brainwave of the subconscious mind where we experience daydreaming and meditations and most light trance and sleep states.

THE SUPER-CONSCIOUS MIND

This connects us mentally to the energy source from whence we came. Our divine essence is expressed as thoughts from within the depths of this part of our mind. It lets us know that we are part of all there is and from this point helps us to remember our divine spiritual nature on all other levels. It helps us to see the deeper meanings behind our experiences of life as we relate all other information from our mind to it. It is where we form a conscience of what feels right and what feels wrong, based on what serves us and what doesn't.

At this level we see that our thoughts are important in creating our reality and accept that we are totally responsible for all that happens to us. This part of our mind helps us to form mental and emotional dexterity. The super-conscious makes us mindful of the things we say and do. We accept personal responsibility at this level. This is the part of our mind we develop when using our intuition and psychic gifts.

God or Christ consciousness is perceived and expressed at this level as we open the doors of perception to cosmic consciousness that deals with divine laws, love and truths. It is from this platform that we experience all spiritual ecstasy and our spiritual awakenings.

Initiations such as the Reiki attunements are mainly felt on this level. Tuning into this level we are able to raise above all mundane matters and use higher mental vibrations to transform our lower thought vibrations.

Dreams occur at this level, as do spiritual awakenings. Our soul and its purpose reveal itself to us when we learn to use this part of our mind. *Theta* is the brainwave of psychic activity or dream state, it is still part of the subconscious state but is the place we are able to do past life regression and transcend time and space. *Delta* is a state of deep unconscious sleep, the kind most people have each night.

These two states form a platform for the higher self (spirit) to enter our lives via deeper trance states. It is also where we can leave our physical body for astral travel during sleep.

SHIFTING PERCEPTION

The key reason for understanding the mind is to help you, the reader, interpret which part of yourself at any given moment is vocalising through your thought processes right now. During a healing session we shift in and out of different levels of mental consciousness. Being able to know which level you are dealing with will help you to know yourself much better.

To recap on the three basic levels: the conscious mind deals with everyday mundane physical things and issues in your life; the subconscious mind deals with your beliefs about yourself and your emotional reactions to all experiences, and the super-conscious mind or higher self brings in a higher understanding of the other two levels, helping you to put everything into proper perspective with more clarity, purpose and love for yourself.

We are constantly shifting within our perceptions about everything all of the time, at least those of us who are open to new thoughts and ideas. Because of this it is impossible to remain rigid within our thinking or beliefs about anything. Everything is always changing; life never stays the same from one day to the next. Because of these constant changes many within our society are going through a hard time accepting the flow of energy that changes bring about. This non-acceptance makes them unhappy with life and they can get sick as a result.

ACCEPTING CHANGE

Fixed ideas and rigid thinking show up frequently as stiff, sore bodies unable to move forward in acceptance of change. Reiki will help all of us accept that change is inevitable and a natural part of life as we get more into flow, allowing change to be a part of our life. This sees the doors of perception shift as new thoughts and feelings can be brought towards those who wish to experience them. New thoughts of self love and acceptance will see many liberated from illness that has plagued them in the past. Allowing thoughts of abundance will see many, who are lacking, receive much in the way of love and happiness.

When the penny drops and we become used to the feelings of new thoughts, which empower us instead of the old thoughts that dis-empowered us, we realise that we are totally responsible for our reality and the quality of our life improves. We decide what we wish to experience as reality and the universe just gives us back what we are thinking in terms of experience. So we are experiencing our own thoughts all the time as circumstances, relationships, and all of life's experiences. This understanding brings with it a profound sense of control and a new feeling of total responsibility towards our life and the direction we wish it to take.

We are unable to blame anyone else for any misfortunes that may come our way, be it chance or fate that lends a hand, nothing ever happens by mistake or coincidence. Herein lies one of the hidden secrets and mysteries of life, that once uncovered, sees many liberated from terminal normality.

Free will plays a huge part in our ability to choose firsthand the kind of experiences we wish, simply by being able to think we activate the universe to respond to our wishes. Negative or positive is simply a matter of judgment, choice and or belief. The saying, what you give out is what you get back, has never been more apt in this concept.

By lifting your thought vibrations to those of a positive nature and letting go those of a not so positive nature, you are healing your very existence and total experience of life as you know it. The quality of your life depends on the quality of your feelings and your thinking.

How We Co-create Our Life Experiences

Thoughts have great creative powers and are our main source of our creative energy. They drive us to experience what we believe we deserve. Actions do not just happen on their own; they must come from a directive from our brain via our mind. Our body is a vehicle, our soul is the driver, while our mind runs the engine with thoughts as its fuel. All of our experiences start from inner desires, impulses, and unconscious urges prompting the conscious thoughts of, "gee I wonder how that would feel," or "I wish I could do that." As we think our thoughts we give them form and validate them with other thoughts until you have had a conversation within your mind about something. What started out as a flippant thought becomes an idea. It may take a few weeks or only a few minutes, it doesn't matter.

This mental conversation is overheard by the universe, which is in total service to us and wants us to have exactly what we ask for and so delivers our thoughts back in the form of experiences to us like a delivery clerk. The universe doesn't know how to judge negative or positive, it simply acts in accordance with our thoughts. So we are constantly experiencing the underlying unconscious things we think and say most often. This is how we co-create our life experiences.

As You Think so You Shall Be!

As you think about this you become aware of the power of your mind and how important it is to have it focused on what it is you feel you desire from a space of truth and love. To feel truly fulfilled in one's life one must have the experiences that bring about contentment through purpose, love, abundance and happiness.

Are you prepared to give yourself all the things you will need to be truly happy and contented with life?

To be able to manifest the things that we wish to change or experience in our life we first need to have some idea what these things are. Getting in touch with your feelings and emotions are part of understanding who we are, what we like and what we don't like. You don't want to keep manifesting the things in your life that don't serve you or discourages your full potential. So find out how you feel about everything so that you will know what it is you really want and what you need to look at changing.

1. Know who you are and why you are here. You are an aspect of the one great source. You have come simply to experience yourself in the limited energy of the third dimension we call earth. As a spark of the divine you are able and have the power through your own free will to co-create your whole experience while here on earth, and all experiences are for the asking. Good, bad or otherwise, you are responsible for all that you experience.

2. Know your true desires. Make a wish list or a goal sheet – one for now and one for the future. These things can change however. This helps you to be real about what you need to manifest in order to be happy, contented and fulfilled. These things will clarify what is for your highest good as an experience, short term and long term. Leave nothing out, even if it sounds crazy. If it is your truth, then leave it. Your heart's desires are the very wishes of the soul. Manifestation is the art of claiming your true desires and materialising them.

3. Correct your thoughts. You do this by aligning with your heart's ability to come from love and speak your truth by claiming your power. Look at what you are not happy with in your life and decide to change it. Realise how your emotions and your thoughts have brought this about in the first place and re-align them back to love. All mistakes in life can be fixed once we recognise them and decide to do something about changing them. Right thought leads to right actions and speed up the manifestation process.

4. Learn the holy trinity of manifestation. This is how we manifest in the third dimension of matter. **(a)** We think the thought. **(b)** We speak the thought. **(c)** We do the deed. Sounds too easy? Well mostly it is! However, there are some areas of self-sabotage to watch out for, such as thinking too much and never speaking about it. Or always speaking about it and never doing something about it following through with actions.

I'm sure you know people who have done both at some stage. If you have done all these things and nothing happens and you experience a block then you may need to look at your true motive for wanting to bring this about. If your motives are not pure or are emotionally driven, then this technique will not work. You cannot trick the divine source.

5. Use the manifestation love triangle. The love triangle, (shown overleaf) is designed to be used for manifesting only that which is in your highest interest and good. The energy of Reiki sends an energy flow around the triangle. The idea is to create a flow of energy from you to the divine source to the goal and back to you. This can be written down and then used either as a meditation visualisation technique for sending or as a burning ceremony. Either way it is very powerful.

The holy trinity is at work on this plane as thought, words and deeds. This is the recipe for true manifestation in the divine sense on the material plane. Once learnt they should not be forgotten as they are the key to all healing processes within.

Now a triangle of energy is flowing both ways from you to the source to the goal and back to you, and from you to the goal to the source and back to you.

As you ask so it shall be, he who asketh receiveth.

If it is in your highest and wisest good for this to take place, it will. That is how divine will works.

You must be aware of the fact that time is not always a prerequisite in your asking for a specific goal, for time is irrelevant in spiritual terms. However, timing is of the essence. All things happen in their right time frame and that is why we experience synchronicity. Therefore, you must be prepared to sit back and wait for your desired goal to begin to show up in your life.

Remain detached emotionally but mindful of any signs whether they are people, messages or promptings you get that may begin the synchronistic flow. Go about your business happily knowing that the divine order of things is helping you achieve your desires.

Think bold and expect miracles because they do happen. When you are in flow with your life they will become the norm.

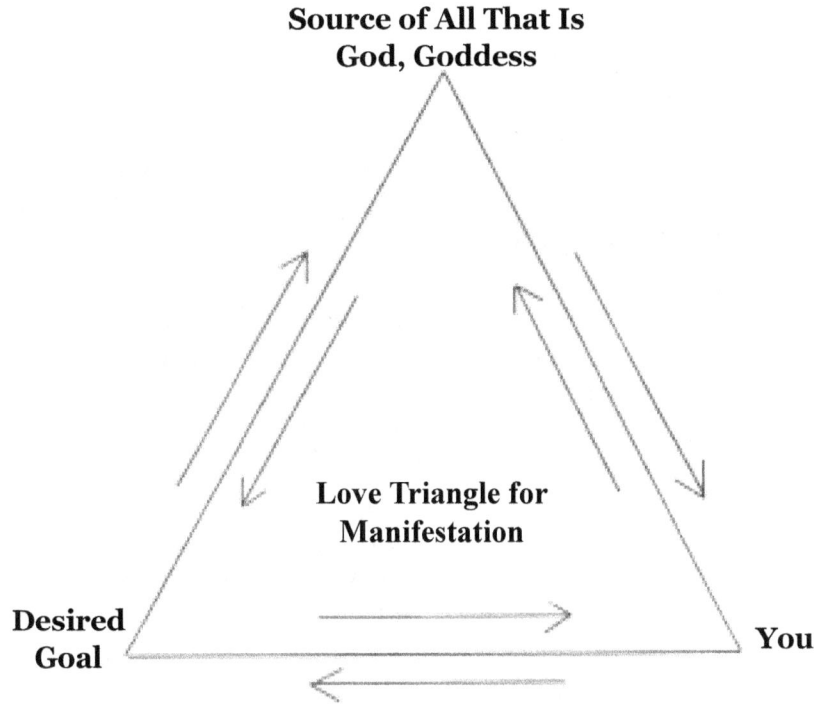

Some Blocks to Manifestation

Self Denial is self-destruction. It gives your power away to others. Know what makes you feel good and accept this as your truth. Decide to only manifest what makes you feel good. Feeling good is your way of telling yourself that your last thought was truth that your last word was wisdom that your last action was of love. Don't live anymore in the land of denial, it saps your energy.

Worthiness is about self-love. Decide to love yourself first. If you do not love yourself then you will not feel deserving enough to give yourself what you need to be truly happy and content. If you lack self-worth you will somehow sabotage your own success if you feel lacking or undeserving.

Neediness. To want something is to crave it. Craving makes us unhappy. The best thing is to want nothing. Simply have preferences and desires but not needs. Know that all your real needs will be met and that life supports your stay. This is important and is a higher state of being and an act of self-mastery.

Credibility. Your desires need to be realistic and believable by you for you to feel that they are obtainable. It is no good trying to manifest flying like a bird because you would not believe this and it will not be a truth for you. You need to begin with the believable. Slowly what you believe will expand as your perceptions shift.

Attachment. This is about you being emotionally needy. Wanting something so bad that it makes you burst. It is invested emotion directed to a specific outcome. The divine may have other plans for your experience so you will need to let go any attachment to a perceived outcome and allow for it to arrive in whatever form it takes. This will be perfect for your highest good. If you do not let go, then prepare yourself for massive disappointment.

Fear of failure is not as daunting as the fear of success. Fears are stumbling blocks no matter what form they take, including fear of change and fear of the unknown. Trust in the process of life and of letting go that which does not serve you. There are much better things for you to experience if you open up to them.

Poverty Consciousness is very common and people with plenty are afraid of scarcity and losing what they have. Those experiencing scarcity are afraid of plenty and receiving abundantly. It is about a polarity consciousness of right verses wrong, good and bad, rich and poor. It believes the rich get richer and the poor get poorer. It creates a world of illusion and separation by placing things at the opposite ends of the pole.

Intention. Your intentions will need to be of the purest kind, to serve yourself and others with only truth and love, to serve self by being of service to all. You cannot manifest on behalf of another, only yourself. This must be for your highest and wisest good as divine will is just that. So be clear as to your motive behind the desire for manifestation. This creates an impervious integrity of right purpose when doing this sort of manifestation. It cannot be abused for divine law governs it.

A Rite of Passage

At certain times in all our lives particular events change everything about us on all levels and we are never quite the same person from then on. We call these rites of passage life changes. For there to be life changes something has to happen to our conscious awareness creating a shift from one level of understanding to another.

In ancient days these times in a person's life were marked by some form of ritual or initiation ceremony and were considered to be a *rite of passage.*

In many cases it was the ceremony itself that brought about a conscious acknowledgement within the person taking part, of the changes that were about to take place. We still have many of these forms of rituals today, which also mark a person evolving from one level of awareness to another. For example:

- Graduating through the different levels at school or college creates an acceptance of attained knowledge.
- Confirmation within the Catholic Church.
- The Barmitsfa is the male Jewish right of spiritual passage within their faith.
- We celebrate the coming of the New Year, marking the passing of the old one.
- Birthday celebrations are another personal rite of passage.
- The burial ceremony is still a spiritual rite of passage for the deceased. The funeral creates an acceptance by the living of the death of a friend or loved one. It's part of the ritual of grief.
- Weddings are a practiced form of partnership ritual.

Creating an acceptance by the couple's statement of a loving commitment to each other, which is then honoured by the ritual and ceremony.

In our Western society we have forgotten why we used to have rituals, initiations and ceremonies long ago. These were special times of the year or of a person's life that were acknowledged by some form of celebration. Some of these more ancient rituals have remained but the true meaning has been long lost in the fog of our modern culture.

The attunements given in the Reiki seminars marks another rite of passage, in the form of acceptance from one's inner spirit of a connection to a universal spiritual energy.

The attunement process is the procedure by which the Reiki Master assists in aligning and balancing the energy system so that the student can become a conscious channel for the energy.

It is the attunement initiation process that is the major difference between Reiki and other touch healing modalities. It is impossible really to explain how it works as it is one of those events and mysteries within our lives that needs to be experienced. Like childbirth it is a miracle of life and one to be moved by.

Seeking after wholeness is the life force's gift to us through this attunement process and one that our nature requires. The attunement ritual helps the impulse towards self-realisation; it indicates the path we must follow, not from our ego motives but from the core of our individuality or soul. In this way these initiations are a profound awakening of our conscious mind as to our very essence, encouraging us to express this essence in a creative way. These attunements are very powerful in making the life force available to us and mark a time for regeneration and healing of the self, down to the cellular level. They create a shift in consciousness and therefore are seen to be a rite of passage.

Most people find themselves opening up and letting light into a part of their lives that has been secret or shut away. This comes about as a direct result of receiving the energy during the attunements. They help open and expand the energy-holding capacity of the person receiving them, as well as clearing and re-balancing the chakras and aura bodies.

During an attunement the energy, instigated by the Reiki Master's use of symbols, travels from the receiver's crown to the heart, and from the earth up the receiver's legs through the lower chakras to the heart. If there are any energy obstructions along this line they are removed and replaced with positive energy. From the moment an attunement is completed a new channel for Reiki is re-born. This energy stays with you for the rest of your life helping you flow back into wholeness.

The Reiki Master is only a facilitator and does the physical motions for the attunements; all else follows of its own accord. I liken this process to turning on a light in a dimly lit room. Attunements are usually a high point for those who receive them. They help take people from fear to love, and thus awaken them not only to their own potential but also to other dimensions and realities.

For most students the receiving of an attunement is nothing short of amazing, even if they are not sure what has taken place they feel terrific and very light. Some are so overwhelmed with feelings of love and joy that they experience deep emotional reactions.

If you are or become a teaching master it is important that you assist your students to receive the attunements by helping them with breathing techniques and meditation for relaxation. This will help with the rising of their vibrational energy, assisting their ability to feel their attunements. In this way they will have a better opportunity of consciously feeling the profound energy exchanges that happen during the attunement process. This does not happen on the conscious level. It happens in deep alpha and theta states of mind, which takes focus and discipline to get to. Spirit will use the opportunity also for carrying out any healing that is required at the time for the student's development. Some students will feel sensations and see colours of varying kinds, others may be visited by visions of deceased relatives and or see past lives. Most just feel a deep sense of love and peace. It is because of this that it has been kept secret and sacred for thousands of years.

I have always believed that the Reiki attunement process was something very special and I have endeavoured to honour this with ritual. I have always burnt candles and incense to help to raise the vibrations, which I have lovingly dedicated to the energy of the Divine and the spiritual masters of Reiki. I have crystals charged with the energy in the room and place Masters Quintessence on my hands evoking a certain Master's essence in consciousness. All these little things honour what it is I am about to perform and puts both the students and my subconscious on notice that something very special is about to take place. The ceremonial use of music for ambience and the Tibetan chimes adds to it all.

It does not matter where you do your attunements as long as they are not going to be interrupted. You do not have to do what I do; it is not mandatory. However, the student will remember their attunements forever, so why not make it a special ceremony for them. It is all part of their rite of passage into the understanding of Reiki. Reiki is a spiritual energy and should be honoured as sacred in this regard.

In the mystery schools of old everything was treated with a certain reverence and respect no matter how simple it was, and so it is that I like to treat the attunement process with this same deference. Personally, I see it as a holy act and one not to be taken lightly. I'm sure all Masters have their own ways of making the attunements a special event for their students.

CREATING CEREMONY AND RITUALS

When students participate in rituals and ceremonies they take part in symbolic passage. It signifies deep change is taking place on all levels. To initiate means 'to cause to begin', or 'to enter into'. It is a process marking a transition from one stage to another. This could be a season, moon faze or level of awareness.

In Level Two I teach a few old traditional ceremonies one of which is the burning of affirmations. This ritual is sacred and allows the students to begin the process of letting go the things in their lives that they feel no longer serve them. It is performed with a reverent attitude and it affirms our individual power to transform and balance our lives. I help them incorporate the use of Second Level Reiki energy, sending to the affirmation before burning. It is a very powerful way to release, claim, and manifest that which is in our highest good to experience.

During the Reiki seminars I like to create small rituals. These rituals help to create a physical level memory of the total experience. This I do simply because ritual speaks to the subconscious mind and reminds it of the Divine. It is the Divine in all things that we fail to see in our modern times and this is why it is so important for us to be reminded. Rituals are symbolic in themselves, for as we create the ritual and get ready for the ceremony we think about what it represents and we align our intent with right action. Mind, body and spirit line up and take note that this symbolises important deep change and accepts the new rite of passage created.

Reincarnation and Karma

It is said, *"That just as man casts off worn-out clothes and puts on new ones, so also the embodied self casts off worn-out bodies and then enters others which are new."*

The concept of reincarnation is not as alien to Western religion as it might appear. Although it is not accepted by the orthodox tradition, it has been a central principal of Jewish mysticism. It was also part of the Christian doctrine until 553 AD, when the church hierarchy rejected it, even though it was implicit in the teachings of Jesus.

Some believe most notably in the precept, *"Whatsoever a man soeth, so shall he reap."*

The *Tibetan Book Of The Dead* considers that the images perceived by the soul after death are not real but projections of the mind. The text itself was written approximately 1,000 years ago and takes the form of readings that are to be recited at the time of death and during the following 49 days. During this time it is believed that the soul hovers in a state between death and rebirth. The purpose of the readings is to allay the anxieties of the dying and to guide their spirits through the various stages that determine whether they will attain nirvana or be reincarnated – another rite of passage.

This book's description of the three stages of death are very similar to the many reported near death experiences (NDE) that have been recorded all over the world by many cultures and varying faiths in more recent times.

The first stage, which the Tibetans call *chikai bardo, is* the moment when the body has ceased to function but the person remains conscious, unaware that he is dead. Which might be described as his astral (or 'etheric') body. The deceased finds himself floating free of his physical body, unable or unwilling to leave the physical world behind. Quite often emotional attachments may cause the soul to linger, especially if it has a strong desire to communicate with family and friends. Reiki can be used to help with this stage of passing over and assists with the spirit's acceptance of the death stages, even prior to death.

But eventually the soul must enter 'clear primordial light'. The assumption is that if a person has experienced the 'light' during life, he will not be afraid when drawn to it after death. For those who are unprepared or still bound by material concerns or ego, this prospect is too terrifying and the soul retreats through a succession of dreamlike states of its own making. This contradicts many recently recorded incidents of NDE in which the dying person recollects an irresistible attraction to the light and a reluctance to return to the physical body.

The next stage is judgement, a common feature of many otherwise differing religions. It conveys the idea that the deceased will be judged by his own conscience and thus creates Karma. *"Then the lord of death will say, "I will consult the mirror of Karma, where in every good and evil act is vividly reflected."* Karma however is unique to the Indian religions. It is the Universal Law which states that past actions have an effect on the present life of an individual and that each thought and action creates an effect in the present or a future life.

CAUSE AND EFFECT

The concept of karma as a spiritual law has been interpreted by many traditions as the law of 'cause and effect'. Karma seems to exist because of some action of non-forgiveness, debt or trauma, whether it is to self or another. It represents the cosmic operation of retributive justice, according to which a person's status in life is determined by his own deeds in a previous life.

My understanding is that for every cause there is an effect, so if your actions are of good cause there will be good effect and you create good karma. Just the same, if your actions are of bad cause there will be bad effect creating bad karma. Creating the statement, "What you give out you get back," we are creating our own karma all the time with our thoughts and our deeds. Karma can be shown in many ways and teaches us the lessons that our soul has decided to learn through incarnating into physical matter. We choose to come to earth to eventually get it right as it were.

Karma can be seen through the many circumstances we find ourselves in such as the parents and family that we have chosen. It quite often shows up as patterns of behaviour and attitudes. To clear this we need to first recognise it, then we can begin to let these patterns of thought and reaction go. This we can do by changing our beliefs and releasing them, allowing our more divine nature to be displayed instead. As we clear away these aspects of self we connect to the higher mind and so reflect this in our thoughts and deeds. We let more light into our life creating better karma. Enlightenment dispels the burden of karma and we are supposed to dispel at least 50 percent of our selected karma before we can be allowed the wheel of rebirth (continual incarnation). Ultimately, we are responsible for our own destiny.

Death is seen by many cultures to be a rite of passage into a perceived better world. This passage we have seen honoured in the time of the great Pharaohs of Egypt. Their belief in the afterlife was very strong indeed. They had pyramids built with many secret chambers with which to place their beloved family and their prize possessions.

We are a part of All That There Is.
A quiet whisper of the one far cr,y
All encompassing yet apart.

The human mind seeks that
Which is known by our deeper selves.
That we are in truth a part of some
Greater Whole.

Our birth takes place beyond the stars.
Our end a mere transmutation of the Soul,
Which seeks to roam forever
Amidst the many reflections
of it's mirrored SELF!

- Michael.

DOORWAY TO THE DIVINE

My family was not at all religious, so the word 'God' rarely got lip service unless used in vain. I had no idea what God was in real terms and didn't really care, never thinking it important enough back then to ask or discuss it at length. I personally had a real aversion to those perceived religious types and closed off on all levels when the word God was even mentioned.

However, during the course of my life and career I had come to accept that a large proportion of the general public needed to hold onto some kind of belief or faith without really knowing why. My feelings about this subject simply reflected my own ignorance. I felt that people used religion like a crux, like alcoholics use alcohol as a form of escape into non-reality. I saw it as an escape mechanism by not fully taking responsibility for their life and any painful events within it. I was not in judgment of this as long as it was not thrust onto me, so I remained an uninformed agnostic.

I considered myself to be a realist not needing any form of religious escapism or dogma. As a child I had attended Sunday school and remembered that I loved the pictures of Jesus and the Angels in the children's Bible. I also remember pictures and stories of Jesus as a boy and then as an adult. I tended to view religion and the story of Jesus as some sort of legend or fable past down through generations that did not pertain to me in this life at all. I put my trust in logic and science, totally dismissing the need for religion or God in my life.

I feel this is the case for the majority of people who do not belong to a religious mindset. I have met many such people in my life that, like myself, did not feel the need to yield to any kind of dogmatic teaching. I have always seen religion as a form of controlling the masses, not really knowing where these feelings came from. However, I had to admit that they existed in my beliefs somewhere.

I remember my father telling me that he gave away the church and religion when they kept asking him to give them money. Now Dad was a proud man who worked hard for his living and would help anyone that asked for it. He found it impossible to believe that the church would want to take money from a poor shift worker who had five children and a wife to support. Disillusioned with so-called God-faring people he never went back to church. His disappointment probably played a large part as to why I came to my understanding about religious types in the first place. That and the Bible-bashing, door-knocking types that also arrived on my father's doorstep only to wake him from his precious sleep.

So you can imagine when first learning Reiki that it was difficult for me to come to terms with the concept that the energy that I was channeling through my hands had anything to do with God.

It was the energy science of Reiki that rescued my consciousness and helped me to accept that God was not a person who sat in judgment over us but an energy, a force that permeated every living thing. This took me a while to integrate the concept that God was a loving life-force energy that affected every living thing. I understood it perfectly. It felt so right and I knew it in my heart as a truth.

I understood what God was finally and it took learning Reiki to put it into an energy concept that sat well within my true feelings and logical mind. I knew that the power of this healing energy was certainly different to anything else I had ever learnt. I also knew that Reiki affected me lovingly every time I used it on myself. I felt calmer and more relaxed the more I used Reiki. In the beginning the study of metaphysics and energy concepts were fast becoming a way of life. Life force is God force, so is love and we are a part of this force, not separate from it.

Learning about Reiki energy can help those of us who have no idea or true knowledge about the energy of the Divine become more spiritually aware. I feel that many like myself have and will find the doorway to the Divine through more metaphysical modalities such as Reiki.

There are many people in our community who have grown cynical about religion and have moved away from the understanding of God as love. The energy of love was demonstrated to me through the use of Reiki and this was the Divine at work. The more I use Reiki the more my spirit connected to the energy of the Divine creator, our God.

I never thought I would ever use such terms in my life, so I suppose I have been transformed into a true believer in the energy and power of our creator. I wonder how my father would feel about that now?

When teaching Reiki I teach it as an energy science, for it is and can be more easily understood if taught this way. Also, it does not threaten anyone who does not yet understand the concepts of God as energy. For those who already believe, they take to the spiritual energy of Reiki like ducks to water. Reiki is definitely not a religion nor is it full of religious teachings. However, those who feel drawn to it usually make the spiritual connection on their own.

The five spiritual principals set out by Dr Usui are in line with people the world over and are related directly to the self, that is the God self or true self. The practice of using Reiki energy on oneself becomes a very personal thing and I encourage individuals to experience it the way they choose or see fit. If Reiki is meant to be a doorway to the Divine for some of us, so be it. This may not be the case for everyone.

I have taught Reiki to many devout Catholics who confirmed that much of what is taught is also taught within their church as part of their way of spiritual healing. I have only had one Catholic friend who felt Reiki was not in line with her religious teachings. This came about simply because one of the other students (another Catholic) asked some questions of a religious nature that I felt needed answers. I was unaware that my friend would take these answers to heart. She felt that learning Reiki was against her church's beliefs.

Not everyone is ready to be challenged by or can accept other people's ideas, conceptual perceptions and beliefs. Interestingly, the other members this particular class were also Catholics. That old saying, 'you can lead a horse to water but you can't make him drink', felt true with my dear friend.

Fear plays a huge part in many people's beliefs and not only about religion. My friend feared that the church, her parents and other family members would not and could not accept this new form of healing that she had decided to learn. This meant that she might be confronted by their beliefs that made hers wrong. She was not ready to be confronted and saw the whole issue as one of possible rejection from people she loved, and could not come to terms with it. Sad to think how religious dogma can get in the way of perception and growth. Yet she had amazing healing experiences during her workshop.

This event was to be a huge learning curve about religious doctrines and perceived family peer pressure. Many are simply not ready to stand firm in what they experience and know to be a truth, at least not initially.

A few months later I was to receive a phone call from my friend who happily told me how she had used Reiki on her mother and brother who both loved it. She had, in her own time, come to the conclusion that these were her own fears. Everything works out in the end. She now wants to progress with her learning of Reiki.

Truth the Holy Grail

Truth is a frequent mind game for man,
A solution for solving the questions at hand.
Truth usually depends on what you believe.
'Tis also influenced by what you've agreed.
When later you decide to change your mind.
Truth has now shifted will be what you find.
To offer your truth is a valid thing,
As everyone has their own truths within.
Permitting others to speak theirs to you
Will help you see different points of view.
Accepting their truth is the difficult part.
For all truths are felt as they pass by your heart.

The beginning of our spiritual journey for some is the hardest time of all. Mainly because many of our present belief systems are challenged with new beliefs and knowledge that requires us to accept without yet completely understanding. When I first came to realise *that I was a Spirit having a human experience, not a human having a spiritual experience,* I was so relieved, anxious and elated. It was a time of growth as my own beliefs took a huge leap in consciousness. Learning Reiki was the beginning of my search for truth and answers to the questions about life, love and everything in between. Life took on a whole new meaning. It meant, in essence, that there was more to know than I had ever dreamed about. As I acknowledged my inner feelings of truth, somehow Reiki made sense to me. It gave birth to a new trust in faith of a different kind, an inner truth.

During the quest for knowledge we begin our search for truth. The Holy Grail of truth is what each spiritual warrior is seeking and the quest takes us all on a journey to the core of our honesty and integrity within. Amongst other aspects of self, the pathway to inner truth seems to elude us the most. I have found many people who, because of their intellect, must intellectualise everything and this includes truths, even their own. Truth is an empty vessel unless it travels through the heart. It misses its mark and loses its depth of power when detoured through the mind only.

You cannot love with the mind you can only love with the heart, just as truth must travel through the heart to land in its rightful place. Reiki helps take us all through our heart.

Truth is a sacred thing for each of us and represents all manner of beliefs and meanings to us as individuals. If there's one thing I've found, it's that honesty with oneself leads to truths of one sort or another. Certainly, inner truth leads to growth when listened to. Why then don't we listen?

There are many collective truths influencing us that are derived from various sources of acquired factual information using our intellect, such as education, government, medicine, law, books and history. Just as there are different cultural truths passed down through the centuries via beliefs, rituals, religion, and artefacts that also influence our discernment about truth. All of these are valid and are truths of varying sorts. They represent a large part of an accepted informational menu, which you may use to derive and choose for yourself what is to become part of your Truth.

What is Meant by Your Truth?

By your truth I simply mean your individual divine essence expressed as identity. Your truth may not be anyone else's truth, but it should feel right to you and sit well in your heart of hearts, then this is your truth.

Interestingly enough truth is directly related to our own acceptable understanding of anything at any given moment. Because of this it is not something that should remain static or rigid, instead it should remain flexible and changeable, which allows for learning and growth to take place. Our truth is only static until we discern the next truth, which will replace the latter giving us a more clearer picture of that which fulfils our life, bringing new realisations, growth and well-being. It makes sense to me, so why do we see so many rigid truths?

Our truths are arrived at through all of our five senses which help us to experience: our up-bringing whether it be with or without parents, our religious beliefs depending on country and culture at birth, our total educational background, the environment with which we live, our personal emotional stability, peer pressure from friends and family, our attitudes about life in general, our gender and sexuality, and our physical bodies mobility and agility. Not to mention our more instinctual perceptions and intuitive thoughts or gut feelings that takes place. All of these influence us on our quest for truth.

Taking all this into consideration, wouldn't it be fair to say that there are as many truths as there are people. To add to this query, we must realise that no two people seem to experience the same thing in the same way. We each arrive at our own versions of truth from within our own mind's interpretation of an experience. In this manner we each have a unique experience of our life as individuals.

Each experience is unique whether it is of a positive or negative nature and is valid. So where then do we seek out truth?

Our truth is quite often derived from how we feel about any given knowledge or experience. By this I mean our emotional interpretation and mental perceptions are taken into account, fuelling our reactions. When we own any knowledge as a belief or truth it stands as a hallmark or judgement for any future event or situation. Challenge the judgement/belief with a new truth and watch as the old one reacts and seeks validation through agreement or dismisses the new information as not valid. In the future it may be found that the new information was valid, thus giving birth to a new truth. The more our truths or beliefs are substantiated by physical experiences, the more we declare them to be a valid truth, even if we have a hard time accepting it initially.

So our truth depends mostly on what we believe, collectively or individually. Truth also seems to depend on what our needs are at the time, collectively or individually. We no longer believe that the world is flat because someone challenged a collective truth, validating it with experience.

Truth is not always comfortable, nor is it meant to be. We often refuse delivery of our truths for fear they may not be received well. Avoiding and disguising our truth for the sake of someone's ego, be it yours or anyone else's, and you risk living a lie. Every time you smother your truth, bowing to the neediness or discomforts of others, you are not being true to your self and them. The act of surprising our truths while trying to meet other's expectations, or keeping them happy by stroking or calming their ego, is not a loving or caring, compassionate act at all. We are blocking the flow of love from our higher selves.

To suppress any valid and truthful information is an act of fear and control. Fear of another's reaction to our truth, or not being able to control their reactions and or how all this makes us feel. Many people exist in limbo waiting to be released from old belief patterns, if only someone would share the right kind of information delivered with love. Healing is being in flow with your heart with truth and love.

Your very own unique truth, if delivered on the wings of love without any hesitation, will be received well (even if it is not right away) and is all any one ever needs from you. To give anything less of us is to remain superficial. Every time we suffocate our truth we are not allowing ourselves to be of service nor are we providing any healing. The truth of how we feel, if it comes from our heart, is what will set us all free from complacency and superficiality. Truth is the pathway to freedom, abundance and love, and allowance of all that is.

Have you ever been moved by something that someone said to you that was so true that you had to take notice, even though it hurt at the time? Didn't it shed light on something you were unable to open up and express, admit to or share with another person about yourself? Wasn't it a relief when you could finally acknowledge the pain and set it free to be replaced with acceptance and love from you to you? Hopefully, you thanked the person for helping to set you free from a burden by sharing their truth with you.

This is what can take place when we simply be ourselves and share our true essence with whomever we meet with love and not ego or judgment.

From one spiritual warrior to another I say to you that truth spoken from the heart is a powerful healer and will always be recognised by each individual's higher self as such.

As mankind is entering into the new millennium and the age of Aquarius is upon us, there is a growing urge, a compulsion if you like, to become more aware, more honest and more open to truth. Discernment is upon us and it is time to step into our truth on a constant basis, bringing it into our everyday issues of life with love.

Learning to listen to our heart, which never lies, rather than our head with it's intellectual doubts and reason based on fear, can be daunting at first. Sharing our truths in our actions and deeds as well as our words and beliefs and thoughts, encouraging others to do the same will see us all liberated from the burden of superficiality and make believe. Let's make real and live in a space of truth and honesty for the sake of our own Divinity, collectively and individually.

When we acknowledge our truth and allow the validity of

another's, we remain on our healing path in service to humanity. Truth is the destiny of the soul's higher consciousness and the place we are all aspiring to on the quest for our Holy Grail.

PROOF OF GOD'S EXISTENCE

Part of my spiritual pursuit while learning Reiki was to seek out some kind of proof of God's existence. What I was to find was pointless with this age-old question and argument raised between the religionist and scientist as to whether God exists. God is beyond the mind; it cannot be rationalised or hypothesised, and it cannot be found by dogmatic assertion in a laboratory on a slide or through a microscope. The 'creations' by God – yes, but the creator – NO.

God is the supreme and Infinite Energy from which ALL is made manifest and from which ALL flows. God is, in earth terms, known also as 'Love' – unconditional love. It is the dynamo that drives everything, including man. Even the mechanistic world of fixed laws and predetermined processes under the laws of physics and chemistry, for it drives the universal machine called Earth.

God is found within self – the inner self, and proof of this existence can only be gained by expanded consciousness, the very heart of our matter which holds that mysterious alchemical process that transforms man, the base metal into the pure gold called 'love' (which is our true God self energy).

Love is the highest and most refined vibration of light energy presently available to man for him to 'identify' the energy, or part thereof, called 'God' which is the source of His being. Over the many eons man has lost contact with his source, and fallen into a much lower and denser field of matter energy – an energy of lower vibration.

Should the scientists wish to prove this 'God' energy then they must change tack and even dispense with their present evaluation techniques. They will not need those for this experiment, which is purely based on the heart centre.

The experiment is a simple one. Some of it may be a little time consuming however. It depends on the individual researcher and encompasses various methods. One of which is meditation. The researcher is in control of his or her time and energy.

More intense are meditational studies with a spiritual Master/Teacher where the researcher may be severely tested by the discipline, or more immediately or expediently, through the methods of selflessness, compassion, non-judgment, helpfulness and loving thoughts. Any one of these positive methods will achieve positive results.

These and many other positive avenues will save the researcher precious time, labour and money. Therefore, this method should be most appealing! Perhaps the only 'cost' might be the loss of pride.

No doubt there are many in the scientific field or with a scientific bent, which would be willing to undertake this experiment. Or would you prefer to study a channelled energy healing science phenomenon such as Reiki?

These simple experiments will be well on the way to proving God's existence. The rewards for anyone who engages these methods will clearly manifest through feelings of well-being and peace with all humanity, a valuable extra indeed! It is the only method that by 'feeling', one can prove the energy exists that we call God.

Many people will query that God can only be found in a church or within a religion. I would ask that they understand, even if they can't accept, that many others within the community do not seek God through such means. My comments are not meant replace their faith, but they could be an added positive dimension and seen as an alternative route to God for those who do not seek Him via that path. People should be encouraged to find the Creator even if not through mainstream methods? We should spread God like butter – margarine if it is more spreadable!

Reiki helps to spread divine energy through love and healing.

PART THREE

The Challenge of Mastership

We are all individuals and there are many reasons for wanting to become a Reiki Master. Many people get their first inclinations about becoming a teaching master from the first time they find themselves doing Level One. Others feel a gradual pull in this direction as a part of their natural spiritual evolvement with Reiki. Or it may be simply a wish to complete an understanding of this energy healing modality and in order to do so they must complete their mastership.

Whatever the personal reason is for wanting to become a Master of Reiki, it is respected as being a sacred part of your spiritual growth as you journey through this life.

The most common reason I have found that most people do their mastership is that they just wish to be of service to mankind on all levels and see Reiki as being a vehicle and platform for them to do so.

Becoming a Reiki Master is quite simply a decision made from the desire to teach others what it is you have found out on your journey through discovering and using the energy of Reiki. Some treat this time as a spiritual sojourn and for others it is more a practical time filled with the knowledge of how to teach Reiki and give attunements.

As many people find that they have a burning desire to find more meaning to their life, moving into their Reiki Mastership is a continued affirmation that they wish to connect within themselves on a spiritual level. Usually once this takes place they then wish to help others to do the same.

Many teaching masters are needed to help lift the vibration of the people of Mother Earth. Many more are going to be required from all walks of life to assist, enabling humanity to raise its level of consciousness through knowledge shared, love and healing.

*I offer the best of my talents
and goodwill, making my place
in the universe a better one.*

It took a lot of deliberating when I become a Reiki master. I questioned my motives and asked for some inner feedback. I wanted to be of service but for a while I was in denial that I could possibly teach anything spiritual, let alone Reiki. I believed that I had to have some spiritual gifts that would set me apart, enabling me to do this, such as clairvoyance or clairaudience. I wasn't able see auras or delve into past lives at the time, so how could I ever aspire to becoming a Reiki Master? All these questions and feelings of inadequacy robbed me of the growth that I needed to help catapult me as a natural spiritual teacher. I needed to accept that I could teach in order for me to step into my true soul self, giving me more direction and purpose on that level.

Sometimes we stand around waiting for purpose to hit us in the face and announce itself without any assistance form us at all. It isn't until we claim whom we wish to be that we can become who we are meant to be in essence. Allowing our heart's desires to be expressed and manifest in our life takes courage and a deep love of self. I feel that to be able to express your true essence in the most creative way and be of some service to humanity is what we all seek to find as part of our purpose.

*I am made whole by the message
of live, brotherhood and freedom.*

Our fears of lacking and of not being good enough are our biggest stumbling blocks. Someone once said to me, "Well, if you learnt Reiki for yourself and now know what you know, then what makes you think that you can't tell and teach others the same?" I had no answer for that. May be I felt that I had to be God if I was to give an attunement or something. I'm not sure, but I overcame these fears, faced my demons and became a Reiki Master.

What is Meant by Mastery?

Stepping into mastery is about you reaching a point of arrival and that point is total acceptance of self on all levels. We spend much of our life becoming who we think we should be, not accepting that we already 'are'. When you decide to become a master you are stating that you are ready to accept self-mastery as a state of being and not becoming. Those who wish to tread the path of Reiki have broken the mold of the accepted norm anyway. This is demonstrated as they seek to reach out for more meaning to their life by healing and learning about the soul self. The path of Reiki sees many learn more about themselves, how to love the self, heal the self and eventually master the self.

*Through the grace of the Divine
I am able to know the right path.*

As a master you must now learn how to 'walk your own talk', this simply means that you lead by example. A master shares who he or she has become with love, truth and compassion with others rather than boast about self from ego in order to seek validation. Being a master of self means not needing to flaunt your mastership. Realising that you have now reached a level of consciousness that is different to others does not make you better than they are. It simply means that you have arrived at a broader understanding of life and self. From this broad understanding you will be able to help teach others who are drawn to your energy what that broad picture for you has been about.

Mastery in one's Reiki career requires continual growth in consciousness, helping produce results beyond and out of the ordinary. Self mastery is a product of consistently going beyond your beliefs and self set limits. For most people it starts with technical excellence within a chosen field and a commitment to that excellence. If you are willing to commit yourself to excellence, to surround yourself with the things that represent this and miracles, then your life will change. When we speak of miracles we speak of events or experiences in the real world beyond the ordinary.

*As I take responsibility I also
develop my strengths.*

It is remarkable just how much mediocrity we live with, surrounding ourselves with daily reminders that the average is the acceptable norm. Our world suffers from terminal normality.

Take a moment to assess all of the things around you that promote your being 'average'. These are the things that keep you powerless to go beyond a 'limit' you arbitrarily set for yourself. Another step in mastery is the removal of everything in your environment that represents mediocrity, removing those things that are limiting. One way is to surround yourself with friends who ask more of you than you do. Wasn't this demonstrated by some of your best teachers, coaches, parents, etc? Challenge is a necessary part of the path to mastering anything.

Another step on the path to mastery is the removal of all resentment towards other masters. Develop compassion and humility for yourself so that you can be in the presence of other masters and grow from the experience. We need to remain open and receptive rather than comparing ourselves and resenting people who have mastery. Let the experience be like the planting of a seed within you that, with nourishment, will grow into your own individual mastery.

Let love be the centre of my life.

We are all ordinary people. But masters, rather than condemning themselves for their 'ordinariness', will embrace it and use it as a foundation for building the extraordinary. You use it as a vehicle for correcting, which is essential in the process of attaining mastery rather than using it as an excuse for inactivity. You must be able to correct yourself without invalidating or condemning yourself or others to accept results and improve upon them. Correct – don't protect. Observation and correction are an essential process to our power in mastery.

Excellence is a state of mind put into action. It requires that we review all aspects of ourselves and look for improvement all the time as an accepted part of our mastery. This will help fight apathy and inertia and keep us stimulated, motivated and develop a personal, fiercely driven philosophy of conduct.

> *Wisdom comes from the*
> *Depth of my experience.*

THE ART OF GOOD TEACHING

There are many things that are seen to set masters apart from their students. This section deals with the attributes of a learning master that need to be honed if one is to be a true Reiki Master/Teacher.

Your students will look up to you, model and mirror you as you teach them what you know. Because of this there is a responsibility and an integrity that must be honoured and exercised. A master needs to be aware of the influence he or she has upon students.

You must not decide what is right or wrong for your students; they must learn to do this for themselves. So be aware how you communicate while giving your students directives and become conscious of its inference and intention. Encourage them to find the answer for themselves, and then offer assistance. It is advised not to play rescuer to students as this robs them of their power of finding their own path.

We, as teachers, need to use the correct terms when giving information. Try not to say things like, "You need to..." or "I think you should..." These kinds of statements 'tell' your students what *you think* they should do instead of informing them and giving them the choice. It is better to offer suggestions with the use of phrases such as, "You may benefit from..." or "I feel this book or tape may be of help..." then add a rider such as, "Try it and see for yourself."

In this fashion you are suggesting, not telling or dictating to them. The difference with this kind of communication is that they are left to make up their own mind through choice about information given. It is an act of respect when you leave the ultimate choice with the student's intelligence. When you dictate to students and tell them what to do, there is no respect or honour.

Try not to indulge the ego's need for recognition or validation by seeking to control your students' thinking. By this I simply mean that the difference between a student and master is simply the level self-awareness and information. Be careful not to make your students wrong when they answer you or give their views to you. Instead, become an active listener and let their information be heard on all levels, and then thank them for their thoughts before you give your feedback.

Your job as a teaching Master is to be good at giving information, which will assist your student's growth. You cannot decide how fast they will grow or how they will react upon the new information. Instead you must allow your students to grow at their own pace.

You may have learnt Reiki a certain way and had certain experiences, however, this does not mean that your students will learn or experience Reiki in the same way, so be alert and flexible and understand that each person receives and perceives information differently. This is what makes all our experiences unique as individuals. We were not meant to be clones of one another. None of us are the same.

As a master you will be required to exercise the caring, love, understanding and compassion it takes to allow your students to be who they need to be with out judgment. You'll observe that your students come from all walks of life and all kinds of religious and cultural backgrounds and they may have differing belief systems to yours.

Remember, there is no such thing as right or wrong, there are only different truths and points of view. Reiki can be taught to anyone who wishes to learn it. When you teach Reiki as an energy science, trust and let the energy help them become enlightened in their own way and in their own time as to who they are.

Teach from the heart
What you know with the head.

Teaching anything involves a certain amount of preparation and ability. Not everyone is good at imparting knowledge and the art of teaching, while it can be a natural gift for some, it is also a learned skill. While I accept that we are all teachers to each other in general terms that does not mean we are all great at giving information.

Teaching is much more than reading out loud from a book or having an agenda of information that you wish to share with others. Good teaching is about imparting knowledge in a form that will be taken in on all levels by students. This requires that the teacher, at least, have some basic knowledge of the human psyche and how it works.

How can we teach anything if we do not know how it can be best received by students? Teachers do not have to be expert public speakers, however, it helps to be able to communicate well. Just because we know something well doesn't mean that we are able to teach it well. I have met teachers with qualifications as long as your arm, however, they were ineffectual at teaching people direct. Their head was full of information but sadly they lacked the skill to impart it to others.

As Reiki Master/Teachers we must be able to work on all levels with our students, mentally, emotionally, physically and spiritually. This takes adept skills, knowledge understanding and practice. Do you think all these skills and knowledge can be gained in one weekend or with an attunement? I don't think so!

I spent a great deal of time looking at how students in Level One and Level Two reacted during my seminars and was forever asking for their feedback. I did this for quite some time before I compiled my *Master's Teaching Manual* or even considered teaching another master how to teach Reiki. How could I teach what I did not know for myself to others?

Becoming a teaching master is a journey all of its own. It is the journey that becomes part of the teaching process of becoming a Reiki Master. The master's attunements do not make a master teacher. There is much more involved. Self-mastery is required.

I have seen many learn Reiki so fast and begin to create other masters long before they know just what it is they are doing themselves. This has seen the integrity of Reiki slowly dissolve as if it meant nothing.

Ego takes over in the minds of many when the term 'master' is placed before them. It seems everyone wants to jump on the bandwagon and be a master teacher, believing that they can become Reiki Masters overnight and that it is the energy alone that creates mastery.

Basic Mechanics of Learning

To help you overcome the differences within each individual's level of understanding there are some facts about learning that you need to become aware of. We all learn through different means. For example:
1. Learning through listening, (audio). Expressed as 'I hear'.
2. Learning through looking and seeing, (visual). Expressed as 'I see'.
3. Learning by touching or doing, (kinaesthetic). Expressed as 'I feel'.
4. Learning more by mental processing or logic, (digitally). Expressed as 'I think'.
There is an expression that says:
Listening I HEAR............I FORGET.
Looking I SEE............I UNDERSTAND.
Feeling I REMEMBER............I DO.

It is always advisable, when teaching, to incorporate all of these methods within your format so that students' learning is stimulated the way that suits them as individuals.

Effective Communication Habits

1. Be organised and have everything ready.
2. Know the outcome or goal of the desired teaching. Explain what is going to happen during the seminar.
3. Use tools to help communicate, e.g., whiteboard, handouts, activities, videos, games and ceremonies.
4. Always ask for feedback. a) Positive. b) Negative. c) Constructive.
    d) Group discussions.

5. Offer your assistance when needed. Do not dictate, order, or boss students.
6. Encourage students along the way. Allow them to be themselves and express this accordingly.
7. Check their progress with feedback and analysis. Get them to tell you.
8. Be an active listener. Check what you have heard is correct.
9. Assess by: a) Looking for reactions. b) Checking for knowledge. c) Feeling the energy of the group or individuals. d) Reading body language and facial expressions.
10. Be flexible with your format and go with the flow, learn to anticipate student's needs.
11. Be HAPPY! Lighten up and make it fun. Life is serious enough for people, so laugh whenever possible.

Most important is the need to discuss freely and openly during your seminars.

Ensure feedback is behaviour related. Who's problem is it? Yours or theirs? Don't react emotionally or take their emotional reactions on board. Ensure feedback to questions is close to any events.

The Importance of Prior Learning

It is important for you as teaching masters to find out as much as possible about your students before the seminar begins. Sometimes it is not always possible but the benefits are greater.

Knowing what your students already know is important because most of your students will be adults:

1. Teaching time can be wasted covering territory that students already know.
2. Adults can become bored when going over old ground.
3. It has been shown that students retain new knowledge much easier if it is linked to prior knowledge.
4. The collective knowledge of the group can be used as a powerful teaching aid.

5. Seminar planning becomes more relevant to the student group.
6. Students with strengths in particular areas can be used to assist the learning of others in the group. (This links with the 'Pygmalion effect'.)
7. Learning is not restricted to the training room or workshop; valuable learning occurs informally during breaks and in other social activities when students relax.

It helps to remember that learning Reiki will help expand the consciousness of the students. However, the statistics show that almost all students only soak up 10-20% of the information given to them on any one day. I teach Level One as a full weekend, two-day seminar with a minimum of 16 hours teaching.

On occasion I have taught 'one on one' but I prefer to have four to eight in a class. My largest class consisted of 12 students. Although larger classes bring a rise in energy, they can be harder to teach. There is always more interaction and distraction with lots of fun and laughter. Smaller classes are more intimate and teaching can be personalised, but they are still lots of fun.

Two-day seminars give the students time to ask questions and integrate what they have learnt and experienced. Especially if they go home that first night and give themselves a self-treat and sharing that experience the next morning. This is a big step for many and the sharing with others in the group helps to validate what they have learnt.

Become an Active Listener

To be able to tune into your students on all levels of mind, emotions, body and spirit you need to develop good listening skills. To help with some basic ones I have included these:

Reflecting. Telling the other person what you think they are feeling, to get positive feedback on your observation of their emotional state. You may say things like:

"You are obviously happy about this project."

"Sounds like you're angry."

"It seems to me you're upset."

"You seem a bit worried."

When you know your observation of their feelings is correct you may get them to expand, thus helping them through an issue or emotion that needs to be addressed. Whatever you do don't force anything, allow the student to arrive at his or her own truth and understanding. Your students have innate intelligence and they are able to solve their own problems or see their issues. These tools of conversation are simply for you to help bring this awareness about.

Paraphrasing. This is when you put into other words what the other person has just said, checking you have heard correctly. In this manner you are giving the student an opportunity to hear what they have just said a little differently. This allows them to change what they have said by delivering it to you in a different form or confirm your analysis of what was said. The spoken word can be represented in many ways and have many different meanings.
You may use phrases like:
"If I understood you correctly..."
"So you're saying that..."
"Sounds like you're saying..."

In repeating something someone has said, both you and your student get more clarity during the course of conversation. Ultimately, we as teachers want to have clarity about what our students are either experiencing or feeling, helping us to deliver the right messages and information.

Focusing. This is where you ask the student to focus on the main issue of their concern. You are seeking out a core issue enabling you to be able to help them. The idea here is to get them to be specific.
You can use phrases like:
"I know all these concern you greatly but is there one of these in particular that we can do something about now?"
"Of what you've just mentioned, what concerns you the most?"
"Out of all those fears you've described which one upsets you more?"

Some students rattle of a list of complaints or issues and it is your job to pinpoint the ones that need addressing at that moment. This method helps you to get to the point quickly and helps focus their mind on one thing at a time.

BARRIERS TO LEARNING

It may be useful to note the factors which generate negative reactions among adult students. It pays to cast your mind back to some of your worst teachers at school and why they were so. We don't want to affect our students like that now do we?

Boredom. Is where students are turned of the subject matter because of the delivery technique: lecturing, monotone voice, teacher likes sound of own voice, reads direct from manual. Ultimately it's the students' lack of involvement that causes loss of interest.

Confusion. If there are no guidelines or explanations given about what is being taught, the students are left to interpret for themselves, confusion sets in and they will begin to fear the worst.

Irritation. Through annoying actions such as: digressing from the point, mannerisms, disruptions, and alterations to program or requirements.

Fear. Fears of failure, appearing stupid or not being able to measure up to standard, are normal adult concerns. Take time to allay fears and reduce anxiety because it can be contagious. Many adults feel that they are almost past the point of learning and need encouragement and support in large doses. Insecurity plays a role in the barriers to adult learning. Helping to breakdown these barriers will go a long way in helping your students to be able to remain open while learning.

Independence. How can you be helpful, warm and understanding, yet help students to remain independent? The best course of action is to help students by guiding them to find the answers to problems themselves, and then you are able to be both friend and tutor. Adults are especially used to their own mind, thoughts and feelings being right for them. Validate their statement and offer some other suggestions or answers by allowing their mind to register other thoughts and opinions. In this way you are not robbing anyone of their intelligence or self-esteem, you are merely adding information to what they already know – there is a difference. If you are continually making students wrong and yourself right, they will eventually take it personally and either resent you or feel stupid. Either way you will be setting up a negative block in their desire to learn from you.

Understanding the psychological factors that influence our behaviour will assist you in dealing with students who have developed negative attitudes. You are allowing them to understand their own behaviour a little better by listening to them while sending them love.

What is Taught During Mastership?

I did not consider myself to be a psychic or healer before my Masters. Afterwards there were many shifts within my consciousness and energy. Now I am a direct channel for spirit and work with higher consciousness from other realms. Because of this I tend to attract like-minded souls who need my teachings to aid their journey to higher consciousness and spirit. This is all part of my Reiki Master's training together with psychic protocol, teaching spiritual evolvement, metaphysics, the process of First, Second and Master's Level, the attunement process, personal mastery, channelling, new symbology, the art of good teaching and much more.

My Master's Level is designed to teach all the attributes needed of a teaching master, however, I like to tailor the mastership to suit the initiate's needs and spiritual requirements, we are all individual.

I am always guided by spirit as to their needs and their guides work with me to help with this process. As a result, it takes as long as it takes; some students span it out over a few months, while others take a few weeks. I charge $1,950, no matter how long it takes. Any further teaching that is ongoing is free and they may attend as many workshops that they feel necessary to experience the teachings in practice.

My first Master took only one week to complete her teaching because she was already a good Reiki channel. She began to receive her Master's symbols after doing Level One. Diacon had done extensive work on herself spiritually and had previously attended many of my workshops. Diacon already understood how and what was taught during seminars and worked well with her spirit guides. She and I still work together teaching occasionally and are very close friends.

During her back attunement she visited the Akashic Records and saw her life. It was a most profound experience for her and I. Her guides were well pleased with her progress. Diacon, like myself, is a conscious channel for spirit. She brings in a beautiful feminine, soft, nurturing Quan Yin and Mary energy.

I believe that Reiki mastership helps to bring about the spiritual healing techniques and psychic giftedness that is correct for each individual and they step into this mastery as they blossom as masters.

SELF MASTERY

Mastering self and allowing more soul to be displayed in our life evolves four main steps.

The first step is to **know** the self. There can be no mastery of self without knowledge from the higher self passed onto the lower self first. When we can accept and work with this knowledge about the self we are becoming truly enlightened.

The second step is to **love** the self. We cannot expect others to love us unless we learn to love ourselves first. Opening your heart to accepting the self is a giant step to self-love. True love will come your way upon accepting love from the self.

The third step is to **heal** the self. By this I mean that we need to look at all aspects of the self and take the responsibility to heal those parts of us that are not whole yet, whether they be of mind, body or spirit by bringing your self into more balance.

It is because of this need for self-healing that we've seen the rise in the development of New Age self-healing modalities such as massage, aromatherapy, Reflexology, meditation, Reiki, Rolfing, Pulsing, Bowen, Kinesiology Orthobionomy and Horstman technique. They are now being accepted as necessary in our society, helping to heal the spirit by releasing negativity.

The fourth and final step is to **share** what you learn and know with others. This is how you put back into society. Every time you share your wisdom to those who ask, you're helping to lift the whole vibration of mankind.

The more we help each other and shed light on those aspects of self that have been hidden away, with truth and love, the more we will grow as a people.

When all four aspects have been put into place then you are truly the master of self. I wish to share my gathered knowledge with those whom I meet.

This has not always been easy for me to do. However, the more I share and teach others with truth and love the more acceptance and freedom I receive within, it feels good so I must be doing something right.

TRUST AND TRANSFORMATION

Harnessing the workings of your mind leads to transformation. As you take control of how you think and feel, you are choosing to create the future with your will and intention, aligned with the soul's purpose.

Seeking the strength and wisdom, through your ability to love, helps bring this transformation into action. It is displayed in your life through the deeds you undertake and the words that you speak. By mastering the self you are able to manifest your secret dreams through the process of transformation.

Loving the self means trusting the self. Without trust there is no love. Trust in the power of love and see the transformation that you can bring about in your life. Trust is opening yourself up with love, not just mental understanding. You cannot love the self or others with the mind; you must listen with the heart. This is the way of the soul and true mastery.

*Don't learn everything with the mind,
intellect can be an empty vessel
without love to sail it.*

Every time you are possessed by an emotion that you cannot control, know that it does not belong to you. Trust the process of releasing your fears and negative emotions with love. By filling the emotion with the power of love and releasing it to the universe, it is transformed. Just like muddy water running to the sea, becoming clearer with every wave.

Learn to let go of these destructive powers that inhibit your growth. Instead, allow your spirit to experience mystery and magic. When living the ordinary life in an extraordinary way, its magical. Magic is part of mastery and what we are all looking to experience in our lives. But the minute you try to hold onto it, you lose it. Out of the mysteries of creation comes the magic of life. When you live your life out of the passion for existence you will find true magic.

LEARNING TO NURTURE AND BALANCE

Harmony can only be found when you begin to find the balance between the physical and spiritual aspects of your life. Imagine yourself in the centre of your body. To the north is your emotional self, to the south is your mental self, to the west is your physical self and to the east is your spiritual self. As you stand in the centre are they in balance and in harmony?

Do you spend as much time in the emotional (north) as you do in the mental (south)? Are they balanced? Reflect on whether you spend more time in your physical (west) than you do in the spiritual (east)?

To function properly there must be harmony and balance within all these aspects of self. Listen to your soul and bring yourself into balance by adjusting your actions or behaviour patterns in all directions. This is the mark of true mastery.

*For there to be true harmony
there must be balance.*

It can be achieved simply by taking care of your body with diet and exercise and bringing a greater awareness to any exchanges you do with money. Protecting, nourishing and loving your family while expressing your integrity through helping society come into balance also. Making your spirit available to knowledge along the path to higher consciousness helps to bring you into balance.

This kind of balance sees you prepared in your physical life for higher spiritual learning. With true balance in your life it is easier to listen and feel the needs of your soul. Learn to take time out and nurture your spirit and heal any wounds that may occur from time to time. Life is about give and take and that includes the self.

Listen to all aspects of your being and when something feels out of balance take time out to do some healing in that area. Learn to see through the social barriers that cloud the visions of men and women alike and nurture the spirit. This is an act of mastery, knowing when to retreat and do without doing.

When you nurture the spirit you find the sacred places of hidden dreams deep in your heart. There may be times when your vision of these dreams becomes distorted. Everything will look gloomy or cloudy. This is a test of will and growth, for it is time of the all-knowing soul to be illuminated. You will start to see the sacredness of life within every object. You will develop true vision and your spirituality will become much stronger, helping you to see past the illusions of fear and disharmony.

As you let go and relax into the flow of life, secure with all aspects of yourself, you will be filled with a sense of calm and peace. This is the gift of the soul that can never leave you once it is known. You begin to bloom when you move with the flow of your eternal soul's life. Searching for soul is the search for wholeness, love and fulfilment with purpose. Those of you who embark on this conscious search will not fail. Your soul is calling from the depths of your being for you to begin to master your life.

Controversial Teachings

I have found that students that learn any form of Reiki in one-day seminars rarely have all the relevant information in place within their own minds. It would be simply too much to take in if they have had to undergo the teaching, four attunements, a self-treat and a treatment by someone else – all in one day!

For all this to transpire on an energy level they would have to be former adepts for them to remain grounded. Their minds would have had forced information overload or lack of supporting information given.

This coupled with the confusion of what is happening during a class does not sound like a recipe for good teaching to me. Many walk away from these classes needing to source information at a later date from other Reiki teachers.

Teachers like myself have had a great deal of fallout from these 'quickie' workshops. While the energy evokes shifts and healing, it doesn't convey what is happening or why. People have come to me after 'learning' Level One in an hour. They knew absolutely nothing about what Reiki was or how to use it. This has given Reiki some bad press over the last few years. I have made my manuals available to other Reiki practitioners and masters to help them integrate themselves with the understanding of energy and Reiki as a practice. It is the practice of Reiki that makes it work for students.

There is a process to learning. Shortening the length of seminars to such extremes does not allow any of the mind's processes to take place or for support to be available from the teaching master. There are many questions that students will want answered as they learn and time is needed to allow for this.

I respect the processes that learning Reiki evokes. The

belief that the energy of Reiki is all that is needed with only the attunements is garbage. Some of the Japanese lineage teachings have up to seven levels of learning. While we in the West may consider their strict adherence to these guidelines unnecessary, it is plain to me that a middle ground should be very acceptable.

Diane Stein again broke the mold when she advocated teaching all three Reiki levels in just three days. I personally find that this lacks integrity on some levels and does not honour the individual's process of mastering Reiki and its teachings nor the master's energy. Unless a person is ready to integrate the master's energy it can't happen for them.

There is a difference between receiving only master's attunements and learning about true Reiki Master's teaching and mastering self in the process. While I respect her love and honesty as she has spoken of having been guided to do this, I realise that some spirit guides have no concept of the human learning process or just what the human mind is able to cope with at any one time in this dimension. Many of our spirit comrades have never incarnated and do not have the understanding of the human processes that is required at this level.

Guidance is just that, guidance. We ultimately have free will with how to apply that guidance and spirit respects this. Learning anything ultimately depends upon the student's ability to cope with new information while integrating it into his or her own mind's understanding. This process takes time, and yes, it depends on each individual's intelligence and intellectual capacity and spiritual development. Then there is the energy aspect, which takes much longer as a new master steps slowly into their own true god self-mastery, learning how to walk the talk.

On an energy level the human being can withstand great amounts of energy but there is a limit to what can transpire and what they can integrate on this level within a single day. I have found that students go through many energy shifts weeks after the attunements. These can surface as emotions, tiredness, lack of concentration, tingling and light-headedness to name a few. At each level of Reiki there are great transformations that usually take place on other levels and master's energy is no different.

I could not imagine the roller-coaster ride that one must be placed on when learning in such a forced fashion. My belief is that they only get to take so much of it in and the rest never even happens.

Running around attuning people to an energy level that they do not understand seems futile to me unless the attunement is to be used for personal healing purposes. Many would probable say that this is helping to speed things up energetically. I have not yet seen any results of this nature. It simply lacks the nuts and bolts and does not respect the master's energy at all. My findings have been that other masters get the fall out and have to fill in the huge gaps that are left behind. Don't get me wrong I am simply relaying my own personal observations and these probably have limits. I'm sure that some people are served by these teachings, but what I am saying is that I feel they are a minority.

MASS ATTUNEMENTS

As an observer of Reiki teachers I have noticed a swing towards attuning people to Master's Level en masse, using a sending technique that attunes hundreds of people at one time. While I am not in judgment of this either, as I feel it may have its place in the grand scheme of things, it will never replace the hands-on attunements and teachings that one receives from a master personally. Many people came to me after having experienced this and said they felt nothing and gained even less and decided to enrol in my Level One class.

The desire to create new masters is one thing but this seemed a bit off the rails to me and appealed to a certain ego mindset. Many people who attended these large seminars had no basic grounding in the understanding of Reiki as a practice in the first place and left believing that they were now masters of it. This kind of generic left wing attitude served to show up the extreme right wing, which is stubbornly fixed. It all helped in the discernment process within the growing and changing consciousness of Reiki as to what serves us as individuals and what doesn't.

It seems everyone has jumped on the bandwagon wanting the title of master. While this is positively an affirmation that we are in fact masters of embodiment and need to claim it in our lifetime, it must be understood that Reiki mastery does not turn up with an attunement. Some people who attended these mass attunement seminars were Reiki practitioners who couldn't afford the high prices that were being charged to become a Reiki Master and saw this as a way for them to achieve mastership.

I felt for them as they obviously had the desire to teach Reiki to others and I agree that the huge fees that are still being commanded by many of the older and more traditional sectors are extreme to say the least. However, there is a middle ground in all this also. Don't sell yourself short just because of money if you are considering becoming a Reiki Master. Money is a consideration when looking for a Reiki Master, not the *reason* you choose one.

I receive many phone calls from Level Two students wishing to further their Reiki and want to know the cost but ask nothing about the teaching involved. I have helped many new masters with the money exchange aspects so that they could learn and they have always honoured it.

I have found that those who truly have the desire to teach and be of service always find a way or enough money to learn from a reputable master when they shop around. The price for master teaching varies the world over and this is a good thing. Check out what it is you will be receiving for your money and have an interview with these masters. I do not have a problem with potential new masters coming to meet and talk about their mastership needs. They may not do their masters with me and that is fine. I simply allow them to make up their own mind. Many of us are just links in the big scheme of things and I accept that totally.

I quite often make recommendations as to other teachings and whom they can ask or go and see to find out more. Through the Independent Reiki Association of Australia Incorporated, which I founded in 1997, we have many different lineages and masters to whom I recommend new initiates.

I recently completed teaching two women their Master's Level. After years of practising Level Two they decided to attend a weekend seminar to become Reiki Masters believing that all they needed was an attunement. They told me how disappointed they were with the seminar, and even though they had taught a Level One class since then they felt they were not truly knowledgeable teaching masters. Their common sense told them they were floundering and needed more guidance and assistance. After they had completed their comprehensive training with me they found that there was a lot more to teaching Reiki and using master's energy than just giving attunements. They were grateful that they had spent the money to learn a complete teaching, giving them much more knowledge and confidence as masters. They were invited to attend as many of my classes as they wished to see how these teachings were applied.

A lady who was being taught by a traditional teacher (at least she thought so) came to me after many conversations over the telephone. It was going to take her another three years before she became a master and allowed to initiate another master. She came simply to complete her training with me. She had already been teaching Level One and Two for a couple of years.

We met and she felt that I could help her. I was not in judgment of her teaching master's methods or the strict adherence to the amount of years it was taking. However, this lady had been attending regular classes for years in order to learn how to teach and was well versed in the teachings.

NUDE ATTUNEMENTS!

I wondered why her teacher was reluctant to take her further. She had already paid these masters $8,000, received no manual or personal technical teachings of any sort. Apparently, she had her third degree initiation in the nude, something I had never heard of before. It sounded all very controlling and mysterious. She was led to believe that receiving this initiation in the nude made it pure.

I do not have a problem with nudity but this was a bit far fetched. Eight thousand dollar nude attunements for a third degree attunement what next? I had to hand it to this lovely lady; she was determined to achieve her goal of mastership at any cost.

Over the following days I shared with her as much as our time together permitted and gave her another attunement (fully clothed).

She cried, as she had never felt anything like it before. When she left she admitted that all she wanted from me was the knowledge of how to attune a master.

Her teacher had led her to believe that I gave 'quickie' masterships and that I would not be able to teach her much. She apologised for her preconceived opinion of me and said how grateful she was. She had learnt more in three days than she had learnt in three years with her traditional teachers. We parted as equals and still communicate today. These kinds of myths are common practice in some systems of Reiki where total control over the student's progress is sought.

I like the master student's to have a say in their learning processes; they know how fast they learn. They have the right to choose for themselves how long this process will take. I have never felt that students wishing to become Reiki Masters should apprentice themselves to a master for years of indoctrination or conditioning for teaching purposes. However, I can understand why it was done this way in the past.

I believe that the pendulum is already swinging back to the middle path in this regard.

The willingness to be a good teacher sees new masters attend many classes to learn how to teach as well as note the reactions of students to teaching methods, etc. We need good solid professional teaching of this self-healing art if it is to continue to permeate all walks of life through our diverse world. Reiki energy has its own way of teaching us, and as individuals we all learn at our own pace and this should be allowed. Just like any teaching, it is a personal journey for the new initiated master who chooses to tread this path. Reiki mastership is truly a challenge.

Charges for Masters Teaching

Teaching formats will vary between teachers. Some teachers like a strict adherence similar to that of an apprenticeship. The student attends all the seminars for years before they are even considered to be knowledgeable to qualify for a master's attunement.

After the induction very little knowledge is shared with the student who generally relies on the time spent with their master to speak for itself. This was the old/traditional method, taking anywhere between three to 10 years to complete and costing from $10,000 to $20,000.

Hawaya Takata set an unprecedented high price structure and one can only speculate as to why. Takata's granddaughter, Phyllis Furimoto, who is currently at the head of my own lineage, still charges large fees and is very dogmatic as to how it should be taught and who should teach it. Sadly, this seems to be the American way.

Radical non-traditional teaching masters simply teach how to give attunements and leave the teaching of the concept up to the individual. They charge about $150 to $300 and take a day or two to complete.

This gives you some idea as to the left and right wings of the Reiki movement and why politics has come into it. I am glad to say that there are many of us who choose the middle path and are in the centre finding a balance between these two opposing fractions.

I am not considered to be a 'traditional' teaching master. However, I still teach the traditional methods in Level One and Two. It isn't until mastership that I teach new channelled symbology and teachings for the new Reiki lineages to help bring in new cosmic consciousness to Reiki.

Many other masters are now doing the same, allowing for inner guidance to be the teacher rather than relying on the old doctrines and rigid traditions. This was worked well in the nineteenth century when Reiki was re-discovered by Dr Usui. Also, Japan didn't offer much room for flexibility.

Learning Humbleness, Humility and Acceptance

To become who we need to be while expressing ourselves in a creative way, sees many of us seeking some form of recognition for the good deeds we are performing. Just like our pet animals that are rewarded with titbits for recognition of their great performance, so too are humans falling into the ego's trap of the need for constant validation. Sure, we all need encouragement and support along the way, helping us to grow. However, the need for recognition and validation is a different thing altogether.

The lesson for us here is one of humbleness. This could be obtained through the acknowledgment of one's inner joy at a job well done, rather than needing to seek external praise and approval with the adoration of others for recognition and validation.

Many spiritual teachers, including Reiki Masters, are seen to be gathering their 'flock' and surrounding themselves with adoration, for just this very purpose. It is the ego of those who feel a sense of lacking that seeks this kind of mass recognition and power. The desire to be successful in whatever we are doing is a valid thing and can be channelled positively so that everyone can prosper and enjoy it with you.

The fear of not being recognised and acknowledged in their field creates a fiercely competitive mind, which is prepared to use every dirty trick in the book to make it to the top, securing some kind of leadership role. This kind of mind-set believes that spiritual learnedness comes in a book or can be bought at a high price or comes with an attunement form a particular guru or spiritual leader.

Denigration of Others

While I may not personally agree with some fast methods of teaching carried out by others, I never denigrate their teachings. All teaching is valid. Denouncing another spiritual teacher's teachings because you do not know what they are teaching, or you disagree with what they are teaching, creates a polarity consciousness of 'I'm better than you' with the 'right and wrong' concepts of thinking. I am still witnessing many so-called spiritually enlightened Reiki masters continually setting themselves up as gurus and watchdogs over their kind of spirituality, claiming to keep it pure and or traditional.

Change and progress must be confronting to these people if it presses their buttons of ownership and control of any type of spiritual teachings. It was this very kind of thinking that created all the religious dogmas in the first place. Humanity needs many types of teachings in many varied forms without regulation or the need of control or licensing if it is to progress at the rate that is now required. There is no right or wrong way to learn about one's own spiritual nature, it simply is that we all eventually learn. It is my belief that all roads lead to enlightenment even though we may not choose some of them for ourselves, we must allow others their free will to choose their own path.

*All roads lead to enlightenment,
how long does it take for us to learn this.*

Who from and how we learn is up to each individual's free will. Each person's level of consciousness will choose who or what is right for them as they will recognise the level of energy or teaching as being correct for them at that time. When they have learnt what they need from one teacher and evolving they are now ready to progress. They may need to move onto another teaching with different energy for their next step.

Some Reiki Master/Teachers are still in judgment of students who do this. It is not an act of disloyalty. Teachers do not own their students. There is always free will and the right to choose. To try to coerce and persuade others to stay or join your group or teachings by means of manipulation or the denigration of others is controlling and fear based and spiritually incorrect.

None of us can control the changes for growth that are needed for the progression of our humanity; it simply cannot be stopped. Our inner spirit will not allow it. There is no need for these acts of control through criticism and fear. We are all loved and recognised in spirit as being one and the same love energy.

It is a human failing that sees many people, while progressing on their spiritual pathway, still fall pray to their own egos in this manner. What we find is that spirit tests the ego time and again with the challenge of change, no matter what level you are on. This helps to develop the inner strength and courage that it takes to remain humble on all levels while growth is taking place.

Let us be reminded of who we really are in spirit and not forget that we are all one and once united from the same source; we are all the same in essence. The only thing that ever separates us at any time is our different experiences and that is one of the mysteries of life. Learn to love it.

Masters, Politics and Ego

During my time as a Reiki Master I have witnessed a great deal of ego within the ranks of the Reiki community. This non-acceptance of the growth within Reiki and the new Reiki consciousness that is emerging has seen feudal behaviour from some. While I personally believe it takes time and that there is a process to learning everything, I accept that others do not feel this way. It is okay for us to disagree and still respect each other's way of teaching; after all different teachers attract different consciousness as students. We all do what we think is right, based on what we believe to be true.

When we learn to be more accepting of others we become more accepting of ourselves. We see the negative and positive sides of their nature, helping us to understand what it is we see within our own nature. Acceptance of others means that you allow them to be who they need to be without the need for judgment or criticism of the things they say or do. This is how we would all like to be treated and so we must treat each other with this same courtesy.

To reach the acceptance of others you need to have love in your heart for one another. Accepting that we all have the negative and positive attributes within each other, and that we see this reflected in ourselves is of great importance. Observation is not criticism. How can we learn what is correct and true for us if we do not observe what does not serve us. It serves to help us balance out the negative side through positive analysis. This is a necessary part of our consciousness, helping us to become more discerning observers.

Observing what creates the negativity in the first place gives us an opportunity through choice to do something to change it. This comes about as a direct result of shifting focus on the more positive aspects not only of self but also of others. When we choose to celebrate the positive qualities of each other we are lending a hand in the transmutation of the negative sides of all our natures. Looking at the greatness of others should not automatically, however, see you put yourself down as a result.

Instead, we could choose to learn from their greatness by adding and enriching our own. Many people reflect on their own lacking when faced with the positive attributes of others. The 'I wish I was like him/her' syndrome. No one has a gift greater than yours and you need to accept this too. In the eyes of spirituality we are all the same, just different by the nature of our individuality. This is an aspect of learning along the spiritual pathway that needs to complete itself soon.

One of the hardest lessons is for us to accept 'all' that is put before us, without judgment. To become peaceful and live in harmony we must accept all that is with unconditional love. This includes the egos of others who do not yet realise that by their actions (which create separation instead of unity) they are still coming from ego.

I am reminded of a message channelled to me from 'Running Deer' who said, "Success is not measured by the gaining of material wealth nor the adoration of others. It is measured always in the effectiveness of what it is you do."

Time is running out and there is much work to be done. This lesson of humbleness must be learnt and now. We all have innate gifts that have been given to us for a spiritual purpose if we choose to recognise them. It is time to get on with the job at hand and stop wasting our time with the unnecessary judgments of other people's gifts. Check your intentions and underlying motives as to your actions and this will be your saving grace. Ask if you are unhappy or disappointed with someone's action; what is there for me to learn from this? It serves no purpose to spend time disappointed with others.

We Cannot Change Others

We cannot change the actions of others; we can only change our reactions. Time is better spent when we see what it is we are meant to learn from one another. Ask yourself why have you reacted to this other person's actions? Ask how you can be of better service to this energy'? If you cannot serve it – leave it alone.

Our higher self will tell us our truth if we choose to listen. It may be that we must speak out our disappointment or unhappiness to another. However, realise that this act, if it is necessary, must be done with the greatest love and motive if it is to be effective and hit its mark and be of true service. Delivering truth with diplomacy is an art in itself.

Criticism is an empty vessel without the discernment of observation, purpose and service. Like the architect who continually builds great castles, only to see them empty as no one wishes to dwell in them, so too is judgment and criticism empty if you are unprepared to learn your truth through observation of self with love in your heart. Humbleness accepts everything and everyone with love. Find your innate gift to humanity and go about this humbly.

This has been what all the great masters have been telling us for eons. You will find that in doing so you will be sharing your unconditional love energy with all those whom you meet along your pathway. When you honour others with love and honesty, sharing your energy, truth and knowledge with those who seek it, you will be attracting the right people at the right time for the right purpose. This is all part of mastery – learning to walk the talk is masterful.

The Question of Money

As teaching masters accept that they must eat and survive in our modern world, so it is that we need to address the question of monetary exchange for spiritual services. Another question arises to confuse the issue even more; how do we feel about charging for our services?

Some spiritual workers have the belief that any work done with divine energy is free so should not be charged for. In theory I would like to agree. However, spirit doesn't pay the rent or put fuel in the car to go to places for healing. My experience with this has been that when there is no mutual exchange there is no gratitude or appreciation.

Hawaya Takata's findings were the same. Giving people free healings can create feelings that there is some form of obligation, and rather than face this feeling they end up going elsewhere for more healing and are happy to pay for it. Sure, you may wish to gift someone your healing talents, to friends and family; that's personal. It's when we allow others to take advantage of our abilities by abusing the generous gift that we should look at what this means. Is it our own lack of self worth that inhibits us being able to charge a fee or ask for a donation or for some form of mutual exchange? Do we not pay the farmer for the food that sits on our table by going to the supermarket? The farmer, wholesaler and supermarket all get paid for being in service by providing the food we eat. You can readily accept this form of exchange for something physical, so why not for something spiritual? It is all the same divine energy feeding us in different ways.

Food is energy that is required to sustain your body's existence and Reiki is energy that sustains the spirit within, helping to heal the mind and emotions as well. You will have to accept payment of some kind if you wish to continue giving this kind of healing service to the public on a full-time basis.

Another question often asked is our time. Do we not value our time and worth? We are made to pay large fees to visit doctors that last only 10 minutes in order to treat some ailments. Doctors have no qualms about charging their full fee full no matter how long the consultation is. Time is money to them. Most other services are the same; you pay for what you get in return.

Do not underestimate the need within others to be able to pay you for the service you provide. Don't you always like to pay for the services you receive? It is an act of self-love when one chooses to pay to have any form of healing, whether it is of mind, emotions, body or spirit. Do not rob others of the self worth that takes place when they wish to pay for the service you provide. It has been my experience also that when people are ready for this kind of healing or learning they are only too happy to pay for it. Didn't you? They will find the money if it has worth to them on all levels.

It is not necessarily the Reiki that they pay for but the time that you give up to be in service providing it. While you are giving this kind of service on a regular basis you are unable to earn a living doing something else. You will have to accept this as being correct at some stage. You may get those who, for their own lack of self worth, will feel it wrong for you to charge. This is their problem, not yours. Leave it with them. Poverty consciousness is a disease of the ego and has little to do with money.

All new Reiki Masters go through this type of contemplation once they have completed their mastership, and there is always a possibility that ego will want to take over and charge a fortune for teaching services, as some have done. Let your own sense of right and wrong within your conscience be your guide on this matter. I cannot tell you what to charge. I can, as a teaching master, be a guide as a result of my own experience. Dianne Stein charges very small amounts by catering to those who are able to pay at that level.

As money and its worth represents many things to many people we will continue to see different charges for the same service the world over. This is human nature. Some people shop at Woolworth's while others shop at Harrod's; the difference is simply one's perception of value and status. I tend to shop around going were I feel good and were I find what I'm after. Price is merely a consideration, not the only deciding factor for me. Don't let it be yours.

GATEWAY TO THE COSMOS

Many of us have witnessed massive changes in the Western style of Reiki over the past decade. That is because there is a cosmic group consciousness that governs healing energies such as Reiki. Its purpose is simply to implement, through those of a collective higher consciousness, the relevant shifts necessary as we all evolve within how we use, teach and heal with these cosmic healing energies, of which Reiki is just one. These changes have had huge reactions from the so-called traditional sectors, seeking to claim their authority over the use and teachings of Reiki. However, the essence of Reiki energy can never change.

It is, after all, a universal spiritual energy that comes direct from source, owned by no one and available to all. The form may be different or even the content and symbols but the end result is clearly the same. No matter how or what is taught when learning Reiki it is the energy that teaches us to take personal responsibility for the health and well-being of our mind, body and spirit.

People come to Reiki at differing times in their lives for many reasons. Many are seeking more than just better health. The energy of Reiki helps those also seeking personal awareness, development, spiritual expansion and empowerment on all levels of mind, body and spirit. Reiki has been taught in different cultures and it is only natural for it to suit the mindset of these cultural beliefs then and now. Changes with in Reiki are inevitable as we all shift our consciousness and keep growing.

Different Reiki Systems

After having read the smorgasbord of information that is available through the Internet I could see many parallels with each system of learning Reiki. Here is a selection of the different schools of Reiki:

- Tibetan Reiki
- Traditional Japanese Reiki
- Reiki Jin-Kie Do
- Men Chho Reiki
- Karuna Reiki
- Ennersense-Buddho
- Raku Kei Reiki
- The Reiki Alliance
- Radience technique
- Traditional Usui Reiki

While each system went about the process and teaching of Reiki a little differently it didn't seem to matter really when reading the purpose. The end results were all very similar. Wording seemed to me to play a big part in the interim interpretations between each system. In other words they were saying the same things only differently, a bit like different religions talking about God and ways to obtain inner peace.

It was clear to me, however, that most systems saw that Reiki was in fact a process of purification through self-healing and inner spirit realisation. Part of this purification was to travel through the heart centre finding compassion and unconditional love for self and others. Most taught that each level took one through many transformations and or spiritual awakenings and that this was the direct result of initiations through the attunement process happening over a period of time. What was interesting was the difference in time span and this I felt related directly to the cultural aspects of each system.

Most systems taught meditational practices of some sort and breathing techniques to help activation with achieving enlightenment and wisdom through each transformation. Each system gave varying techniques and differing and similar symbols as tools of their particular method. It helped to reiterate to me that symbology is simply the mechanics or tools used purely to help us activate and connect with this vibration and must remain inferior to the energy they are able to help us generate.

I found all this to be very interesting and it served to confirm that Reiki should have freedom to unfold and evolve to fulfil its true purpose for all of humanity. The source from whence it came must have known that it would not stay the same upon giving it to a people who use free will for expansion and growth

The Changing Face of Reiki

Many have experimented with this energy seeking to use it in different ways other than the way it was taught to them in their original Reiki classes. It is because of these pioneers that we now see new forms of using the energy of Reiki. It is obvious to me that there is no limit to the use of this energy if one is prepared to explore the rest of its potential.

Many Reiki Masters have opened themselves up to higher levels of consciousness as part of their personal development and allowed themselves to receive extra guidance, healing and teachings of this loving energy. There are those, however, who sit back in judgment and are content with what they know to be Reiki, guarding what they feel to be pure, sacred and traditional and not wanting to see or accept any new concepts and changes. Others are prepared to blaze the pathway into the future using their intuition, guidance and ingenuity. Sadly they fall prey to ridicule, doubt and reason from these others. It is our right of free will that has seen humanity develop many new technologies in all fields for the use and betterment of mankind.

Some of the things we now take for granted were considered to be foolish and stupid originally. Take electricity for example, an energy that we now worry about not having.

During times of change there is always uncertainty as we journey forward into the unknown. People who are fearful of new things or change in any form look to anchor themselves with what is familiar and known. This has been mankind's struggle within its acceptance of different religions and cultures and technologies the world over.

The consciousness of our Western society is evolving at an enormous rate at this time. Cultures worldwide are experiencing major shifts in political, economical and spiritual perceptions, needing desperately to move on from a past that no longer serves the masses in the now. Each culture has been guilty of blindly accepting 'authority' as being the only source of truth. This is being superseded as individuals the world over are seeking to find their own path to empowerment by taking responsibility in all areas of their lives. We need to accept that we are God incarnate and are able to know directly from within what is right true and holy without seeking another intervening source to tell us.

There is a burning desire within all humanity to find its true destiny and look for a higher purpose for existence. Because of this, many people are looking outside the accepted 'paradigms' of science and religion within traditional cultures for these answers. This is causing a great deal of pain and agony as the authorities clamp down on anything that threatens their existence or power. They use force to stop the masses from changing or taking back their power.

We see this too within the realms of Reiki. During cultural or personal changes of this kind there is often a certain amount of emotional/mental stress if there is resistance to change by those who seek to impose their will and beliefs onto others.

Pain in any form is only a symptom of some kind of resistance to a new sensation, idea, emotion, feeling or challenging new belief. Metaphysical healers should be most aware of this. Isn't this what we are dealing with during our Reiki healing sessions – helping people to move on from what is no longer serving them energetically on any level? Reiki is empowering the masses to take responsibility for something as simple as their health and well-being.

I may not teach some of the other forms of Reiki as I do not know them and haven't come in contact with them, but I recognise their merit and totally respect those who choose the right to teach them.

I applaud those who are brave enough to channel new techniques, blazing the path for the rest of us to follow their example without judgment. My hope is that there are many more. The state the world is in at the moment it can do with all the help it can get. Reiki forms an excellent bridge for individuals to walk across safely helping to find themselves and their destiny at their own time and place no matter what that is for them.

If you are already a Reiki practitioner then please don't seek to limit Reiki or its form. We need diversity like we need the air to breathe. It is in humanity's nature to experiment and break the rules of tradition to grow and expand beyond limited beliefs. Nothing new was ever learnt by staying the same. It is a law of nature that demands things must and do eventually change to grow.

New Consciousness of Reiki

During my own Master's teaching in 1996 with my mother, Dr Usui came in spirit through a trance medium channel who was also doing her Master's. She told us of changes that would be coming to Reiki. Usui channelled new symbology to my mother before she even did her own mastership with Mackenzie Clay, and continued to do so after. I now teach all new Cosmic symbols at Master's Level. Mum was told that these new symbols would be among many that would see a shift into a new vibration that would bring a new consciousness to those who use Reiki.

One of the symbols channelled to her was fearured in Dianne Steins *Essential Reiki*. It was the non-traditional *Dai-ko-myo*. My mother had been given the very same symbol long before we ever saw it elsewhere. This was confirmation for us both about the synchronistic events that happen to those who tap into group consciousness and who listen and act upon what they are given from these spiritual hierarchal groups who oversee this dimension.

These new symbols speed up the processes of healing and progress students within their own consciousness much faster. I believe that true masters of this healing art are given symbols that help to bring in a vibration that suits their own energy or which connects them to a particular vibration for the purpose of healing and enlightening others and themselves.

Many other Reiki Masters have been guided in this manner also.

You may make of this what you will, for there are many teaching masters who are not working with or connected to spirit and who are not working on this level of cosmic consciousness. I have witnessed many masters who are locked into their own ego and don't create other masters. I was always led to believe that true masters create and encourage others to step into their own mastery letting it take whatever form is correct for them without judgment.

OPENING TO CHANNEL

Becoming a channel is one of the steps to becoming a Reiki Master. For some it happens as a natural progression during their mastership. It marks the beginning of learning direct from their own spirit guides. Channelling simply means that you become a conduit for higher levels of consciousness. It is the ability to plug into spiritual hierarchy, angelic realms, Ascended Masters and other inter-dimensional beings for the purpose of receiving guidance and profound communications.

This can be achieved when you learn to shift your energy vibration up a few notches. It's not as hard as it sounds. Many have begun to channel simply by using Reiki energy for healing. We are all opening to channel the minute we learn Reiki, so it is only natural that it would eventually progress to consciously being able to channel the highest spiritual realms of love and light.

Contacting the angelic or spirit world has connotations of being New Age hippie- type moon cookies. My belief is that it will become commonplace for all to remember how to do this in the future.

There are many different types of channelling and they range from day-dreaming; dreaming while asleep; intuition; clairvoyance and clairaudience; astral channelling; inspirational channelling, just to name a few. Twelve states of channelling are shown below.

I would like to dispel some myths about channelling and about who can or can't channel. Everyone can channel! From simply having a bright idea that is unconsciously inspired to conscious awareness of communication with a being of light or spirit.

As you progress with Reiki profound new things will began to happen to you. Firstly, you will become aware of different energy shifts within yourself during healing sessions and within others whom you will help heal also. This is par for the course as you open to channel because you need to get use to feeling different energies. You begin to see the physical body as a vehicle for energy more and more.

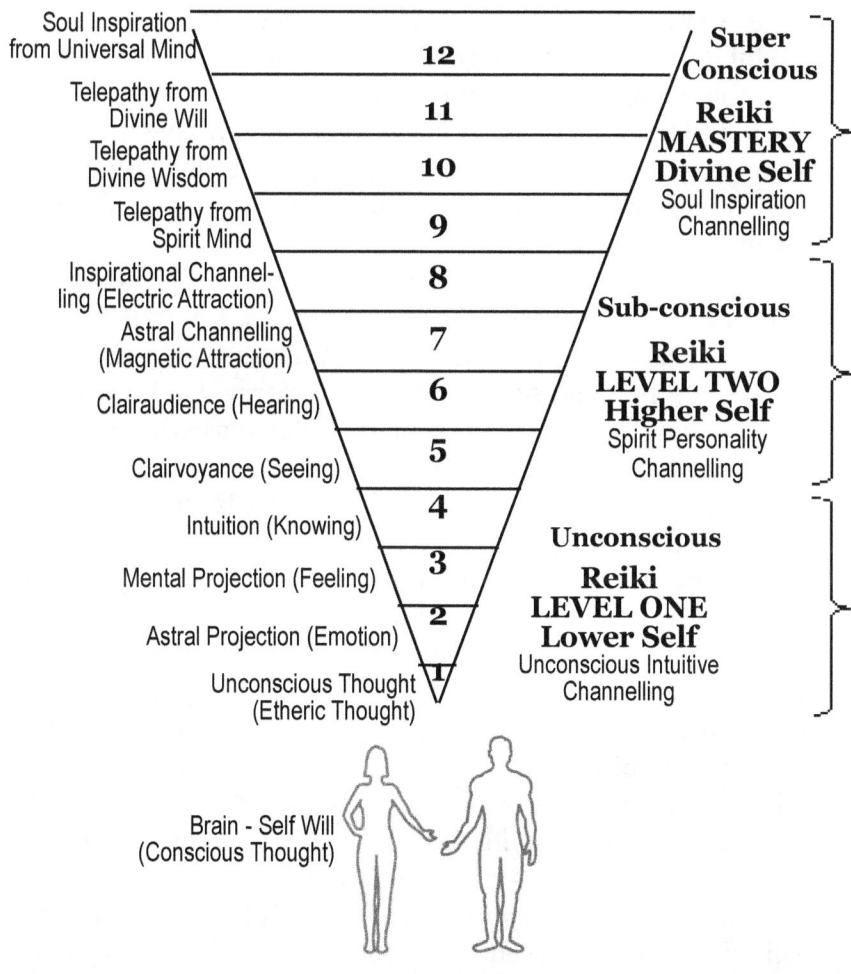

The Self

As you progress your, body can become more and more sensitive to all kinds of energies. For me this meant giving up the drinking of alcohol and eating rich, fatty foods and meat. I was not a vegetarian and being the good Australian country girl that I am I was quite partial to the odd glass or two of wine and a steak.

Becoming a healing channel holds with it a lot of responsibility, which should not be taken lightly. Alcohol and fatty foods pollute the body making it heavy and impossible for some to keep their vibrations pure and channel clear, allowing energies to come through. Makes sense doesn't it? As we shift our vibrations to higher frequencies we will feel the need to let go of denser food and toxins that inhibit this. Many messages I have received from spirit guides discuss this as well as self-maintenance.

We are all natural channels for life force energy. That is how we exist. If we were not, then we would not experience life itself. From the day we are born our higher self allows energy to pass through our 'I am Centre' or pranic tube.

Situated in the centre of the brain is the pineal gland, which resembles an eyeball with the lens facing upwards. This is the highest frequency energy-receiving point within the crown chakra. This is where we interpret and synthesise light or energy that is being fed constantly to us from our higher self. It is what makes our physical body a transducer of consciousness energy. It enables our higher consciousness, which connects us with 'All That Is', to channel life force energy to the body constantly.

The crown chakra and the pineal gland provides us with a mechanism for higher dimensional consciousness (spiritual hierarchy) to be converted from its high energy rate into our lower third dimensional energy and its reality via the physical body through the vehicle of the mind. Once we receive this energy it is able to use our voice and thought processes to convey messages to us. This is where we receive guidance, acknowledged by our minds energy and intuition. You literally become a conscious medium for spirit to enter the physical third dimension.

As a conscious Reiki channel we are already bringing through a specific higher vibrational energy frequency for healing through this crown chakra. It is drawn down from the crown through the heart to your hands and out into the person receiving. Is it any wonder that the next step on the ladder for the Master's Level would be to open up to channelling higher vibrational energy consciousness directly, which by the way, helps to lift our own? Reiki Mastership is a gateway to the cosmic energies for many.

This takes time to perfect and does not happen overnight (nothing ever does). It took me a few years to progress to being a channel for healing before I was ready to tackle channelling of this nature. I was a little fearful at first, as we all are when we begin something new and unknown.

It was the search for more direct and clear guidance that kept insisting that I try to channel consciously. It started when I would get thought forms come through into my mind about the person I was helping. These thoughts turned out to be messages or guidance of one kind or another. It is subtle at first, but the more you channel and trust the better and clearer the guidance will become. You will begin to realise that you are becoming a casual clairaudient and clairsentient.

Basic Tips on Channelling

1. To hone this skill takes practice and we do this with pranic breathing and meditation. While pranic breathing you will be taken through a few levels of meditation to help lift your energy vibrations, which allows for higher energy consciousness to flow more easily.
2. You may feel very hot as the energy begins to build.
3. You may feel heavy or light depending on the energy.
4. You will need to direct the energy to align with yours helping to make it easier.
5. Ask the energy to step into your aura and come closer.
6. As this happens you may feel tingling or twitching and strange sensations, it is okay, don't worry this is all part of getting use to another energy entering your own.
7. If you are feeling comfortable ask the energy to step closer and closer into your aura.

8. Your mind may be racing at this stage with excitement or anxiety, so ask your mind to settle and send it the message to relax. Surrender yourself with love to the energy.
9. Ask the energy to identify itself. This it may or may not do in the way of thought transference. So do not worry about a name if it is not forth coming; it come be later.
10. You may ask if it has a message it would like to give you.
11. Allow your mind to clear as you wait, relax and feel the energy.
12. Try not to edit anything that comes into your mind, your first thought would be that of the energy.
13. Open your mouth and let the words spill out no matter how you think they sound. This is an act of surrender.
14. Usually the words come in short phrases that seem not to make sense until they are strung together into a sentence. The conversation seems to be jerky or slow, do not worry all is fine. This is why you are asked not to edit anything with your own thoughts.
15. Try to always have someone present, either writing things down or taping what you're saying so that you can listen to it or read it afterwards. You'll be able to discuss the sound and kind of energy it was with another person.
16. To close the session with the energy all you do is ask it to leave your aura, as you must close. Give thanks for its divine communications with you.
17. Practice makes perfect. There are no short cuts with this kind of work. You will learn best through experience.

My first attempt at channelling will always remain special. Any doubts that I had left about life after death vanished as I felt the energy of another spirit enter mine. It was a profound experience for me as I am sure it is for all those who experience it.

My whole voice pattern changed. It was the voice of a male with a foreign accent. I was told by people who were present that my lower jaw seemed to change configuration, as did some of my facial features. I was quite conscious of the energy shifts taking place within my body as the energy moved closer into my energy.

Allowing this to take place takes trust. You must surrender

yourself on all levels for the highest good for all that is.

Why would you want to put yourselves through this? Quite simply I feel as teachers of an energy modality we can be of service to humanity by allowing the higher mental frequencies of mankind's consciousness to keep evolving.

Mankind has been experiencing some amazing shifts in its collective consciousness. We are evolving from the Age of Pisces into the Age of Aquarius. That means the ending of the Pisces consciousness, which was one of group belief systems and consisted of low-vibrational ego-based consciousness. Its purpose was to allow mankind to evolve by experiencing this energy. Through these ego-based beliefs we experienced fear of punishment, pain, ignorance, danger, scarcity and separateness through individuation. Those were the old ways.

We have moved into the new Aquarian consciousness, which is a more *individualised* consciousness. It allows everyone a personal experience of his or her own unique individual spiritual essence. It allows them to step into their true power as a co-creator of their own reality, experiencing now the feelings of connectedness, at oneness and absolute harmony with all things in a conscious form.

Having handed myself over as a conscious channel in service as a Reiki Master to humanity I am happy to help others do the same as well as teach what I have learned. It is my belief that we all have these abilities, as we are all equal. I had to learn how to do this, just like I had to learn to read and write and drive a car. You can too.

A Simple Technique

Relax your mind, body and spirit by meditating for about 10 minutes before you wish to begin to channel. Come out of your meditation but not completely; stay with the feeling and energy. Pranic breathing is the easiest way to help lift your vibration. Remember to halt at the top and bottom of each breath for a count of 5 to 10, this helps to slow the breath and breath deeply. Take yourself back into a meditative state using pranic breathing.

Breathing. Inhale as slowly as comfortable, breath white light into your body, filling continuously from abdomen to diaphragm to chest. Rest a moment at the top of each breath.

Exhale as slowly as comfortable, empty breath continuously from abdomen to diaphragm to chest. Rest a moment at the bottom of each breath. Slow your breathing down and keep breathing for a count of up to 10 breaths. This will help take you up into Theta, the state of mind you need to be for channelling. For some this takes practice.

To Connect. Surround yourself with unconditional love and breathe in pink light, letting go of all earthly thoughts and concerns until you are settled. Use Saint Germain and his Violet Fire of Light and Archangel Michael with his Sword of Light if you wish. Ask for your 'I AM' presence to surround you; invite your master guides and angels to join you in divine service.

Statement of intent. Say, or send words in thought forms, three times:

"I AM a clear and perfect channel for the highest realms of love and light of All That Is for only the highest good of all. I AM."

This will ensure that you do not tap into or invite lower vibrational energies to come through. We only wish that the highest forms of love and light be allowed to assist you.

Recall breathing process.

1st Breath In: Visualise a shaft of white light entering your crown chakra (top of head).

1st Breath Out: Expand your aura as you breathe out through your heart chakra.

2nd Breath In: Visualise a shaft of white light entering your crown chakra.

2nd Breath Out: Expand your aura as you breathe out simultaneously through your heart chakra and throat chakra (or the chakra related to the activity you intend, e.g., throat for vocal channelling, hands for healing, third eye plus throat for clairvoyance or tarot reading, etc.)

3rd Breath In: Visualise your guidance, in whatever form feels best for you, entering in the shaft of white light through your crown chakra. Feel and sense the presence of energy. You may feel energy shifts taking place in you body; ask for them to be aligned with you, in harmony with you.

3rd Breath Out: Expand your aura as you breathe out simultaneously through the same chakra combination as Breath 2.

You may connect quite quickly. However, if the connection is not clear, wait and continue with more pranic breaths. It may be easier for you to have a friend read this out to you in your meditative state, helping you to make this connection. Practice makes perfect.

After having done this for a while you will be able to channel quite easily while sitting at a computer or desk to write. The more you practice the better you will become. Have some questions in mind for when you connect, otherwise you will be too excited and forget what it is you are doing this for. Remember, these masters in spirit wish very much for you to connect with them and will assist if you ask them to.

A Channelled Message for new Masters

The Journey into self-mastery is a sacred journey undertaken by the higher self to further the conscious learning that is required for your soul's evolvement. It is undertaken with the knowledge that true mastery must be tested and worked for. It requires discipline and courage, trust and faith. These are the things that, at this level, will be tested within you.

Do not be dismayed if you stumble and fall every now and then. It is all part of learning. For how can one become strong if one does not know of weakness? As you work with your weaknesses they become your strengths and this is the knowing or wisdom that you will share with others that you teach. As you share what you have experienced as your truth, others will gain understanding about their own. They will hear the vibration that only this kind of truth shared with love can offer when spoken.

As masters your spiritual development takes on new perimeters and new heights. You will feel a quickening in your step as your vibration shifts. It will become more and more important for you to maintain your peace, love within and energy levels, through relaxation, meditation and contemplation.

Don't forget to nurture yourself on all levels. Feed the soul, the Body, and the Mind all that it needs to be whole. Do not deny yourself your heart's desires. Do not suppress the longings of the soul. Let your heart dictate your every knowing, feeling and thought. Give your heart license to free think from the soul.

Be in love with your life and all its experiences will become enriched with the glory. You can, as masters, now create heaven on earth for yourselves. Be content with what you can do and do not dwell on the feelings of inadequacy that see you try to be everything else. Be whole and be happy with all that you have already and allow everything that is meant to be yours in the form of knowledge, love or material gain to flow to you. That which is meant to be will come as a natural consequence of your existence. Be content to just do what is required in the now and let tomorrow come. Time is immaterial and does not exist on the spiritual path. And yet timing is of the essence. Chance meetings, coincidences and fate are working in your life the entire time letting you know that the divine is at work in your life.

As you open up to your soul and your spiritual path much will unfold that will see great change within you and without. It will enliven you and motivate your spirit to do what is required by you. Do not doubt your importance in helping others evolve. It is a requirement that those who lift themselves into the higher vibrations allow themselves to help others move into new vibrations of consciousness. This can only be done by the sharing of energies, be they love, knowledge or healing.

To be of service requires that you remain open to those who come to soak up what you have to share. This is why we ask that you look after your own vibration first. Maintenance will be a part of your spiritual path. Develop the love and self-discipline it takes to keep up the level of work that you are required to do for yourself. For if you cannot love yourself enough to do this, it will see your energy deplete and you will not be able to be of service; you may even get sick, so take care.

Always at every level there are sacrifices to be made. At Masters Level one that seems to be of main concern is that of moving into higher consciousness. While most of you celebrate this it requires that your mindset move on from others and can see you feel a little isolated from the masses on certain levels. It is because of this that regular meetings are going to be required of like-minded souls to help validate, bond and make connections for the purpose of helping and supporting each other at this level. Mainstream mindsets are not able to, at this time, to understand or support those of higher vibration in consciousness. In fact, many feel threatened by the changes and are frightened by them. Do not let their fears dissuade you from your chosen path! Instead blaze the path with faith and trust so that others will follow in your example. True masters lead by example and achieve much in the way of greatness simply through being who they are.

You have the ability at this level to affect the environment through people and places that you visit. Simply being in your energy consciousness, which is now of a high vibration, can effectively bring about change. This change will be subtle but will be felt on many levels. It will be felt through feelings of upliftment, the dissipation of fear, and the all-encompassing love that will emanate through you to all.

Mastership requires that you leave behind the old and accept the new with each new day. Nothing ever stays the same, everything is always in perpetual motion moving forward. Whenever we stop growing we are moving backwards, creating conflict with our very nature.

Go in peace and love. Be masterful.

Kathumi

Independent Reiki Association

During the course of my early mastership I began to feel the isolation by others in my field. I felt that having chosen to become a Reiki Master I had upset the apple cart in some way. In fact, they were downright rude to me and I felt that this was not good Reiki behaviour. This was ego and fear of competition at work. For a while I was saddened and then I got angry at the persecution through ignorance. I asked for guidance as to how I could serve this energy.

'Through love and by example' was the answer I received. I realised the only way to serve negative behaviour was to do the opposite with love. I wanted to show unity to other masters by sharing myself with them. I began talking to other people in the Reiki community who had experienced the same thing. They, too, had felt cast adrift as I had.

It appeared that once one became a Reiki Master you were on your own. My mother had found this also but had ignored it, but I couldn't. Something was calling my immediate attention. This fuelled my desire even more. How could this be? Where was the support for a newly initiated master from their peers? It didn't exist.

The birth of the Independent Reiki Association of Australia Inc. was originally conceived from this need within the Reiki community for more unity and less politics. The Association was registered in 1997 as a non-profit making organisation and I became its founding president.

It was the first open association of its kind in Australia, designed to unite all lineages of Reiki practitioners, not just masters. We realised that this unity, if it was to spread nationally, needed to be based on love and not fear, acceptance and not control. We then designed the Association's philosophy around these beliefs.

The Association's Philosophy

1. To honour the five spiritual principals of Reiki.
2. To cultivate non-judgment of everything and everyone within the Reiki community.
3. To create feelings of unity and belonging with all Reiki practitioners.
4. For there to be true peace and harmony we must accept All That Is with love.
5. To place a higher value on learning from inner guidance, rather than just teachings from authority.
6. To accept each challenge and seek to serve all members of the Association with love.

The Association's Purpose

- To unite all Reiki practitioners and teachers throughout Australia with love and acceptance of all, regardless of lineage or organisation.
- To see our individual differences put aside as we share our feelings, experiences and teachings without the need for judgment or fear.
- To promote the cooperation between Reiki practitioners and teachers on the journey of self-healing through the use of Reiki.
- To acknowledge the value of each practitioner and teacher's experiences and knowledge regardless of whether their teachings are considered traditional or modern.
- To help create a level of integrity by establishing a code of ethics and an accepted minimum standard for the teaching of Reiki. (It is necessary to have a code of ethics and basic standards if membership of this Association is to have any value, also for Reiki to gain credibility with the general public.
- To hold forums of an unbiased nature eventually in every state. For members to link up in support of each other willingly sharing

their truth, wisdom and love for the purpose of evolvement within Reiki.
- To keep established a national Reiki magazine, which researches new information about all facets of Reiki.
- To teach Reiki as a vehicle which is used for the expression of love, being the highest goal towards wholeness and healing self and the planet.

The Association had its own magazine, called the *'Reiki Voice'*, which sourced new information, helping to enlighten others through the sharing of information and was free to members. It seeks eventually to hold meetings and forums regularly spreading the word of unity with loving support, offering information to those in our Reiki community who need it.

Reiki Masters' Retreat

I connected with and made many friends with other Reiki Masters through the Association as I pioneered the way by holding an annual five-day live-in Masters Teaching Retreat at Coolum Beach. These were designed to encourage the sharing of teachings and experiences that unite us as teachers of this ancient healing art. It has been one of the most rewarding things that I have done for Reiki besides setting up the Association. There are those who are guarded about what they teach believing that it is superior to others. The Retreat lifts the lid on the insecurities about this and myths of Reiki mastership. We get masters attending from all over Australia as well as from overseas. It has been a great source of learning and growth for many.

All Reiki Masters teach much the same thing with just different approaches, a bit like teachers in our own schools. Personality plays its part and the journey that each master takes creates individuality as well. We can only teach what we ourselves have learnt but if we are keen and prepared to listen to others, we can gain insight into their wisdom and take what we need from that also.

The Association ran for a number of years in the late 90's until I was called to go elsewhere. It helped many to step up and feel supported while they got their Reiki Master Teaching legs. It served by uniting masters, helping them to feel supported dissipating any insecurity and feelings of confusion. It was uplifting and motivating and a special time of inner connection was had by all! Many long term friendships were forged as we laughed and cried together sharing our journey with this amazing energy. I felt honoured to have been able to assist in such a simple manner, and put back to an energy that had given me so much.

Reiki and Shamanism

Shamans, in the traditional sense, were usually found in the more ancient indigenous cultures of our world and still are today, even though the rise in modern medicine has all but seen them disappear.

They were considered to be the medicine men or women of the time, handing down knowledge of herbs and plants as well as spirit. Shamanism was supposed to be one of the world's earliest and most widespread religious traditions. Shamans conducted spiritual healings and were keepers of spiritual knowledge and law and their roots extend as far back as the Palaeolithic era. Remnants of traditional shamanism can still be found today in Siberia, the United States, Mexico, Central and South America, Japan, Tibet, Indonesia, Philippines, Aboriginal Australia, Mongolia and Nepal, just to name a few.

The underlying notions of traditional shamanism are that the world was alive with gods and spirits in nature, as plants or animals, and the supernatural as spirits and souls. The shaman's role was to divine the presence of illnesses, negative energies or spirits that may have been the cause of an illness. In this way the shaman was an intermediary between the natural and metaphysical worlds, able to meet, if necessary, spirits on their own territory. Their healing abilities usually consisted of going into altered states (trance), contacting the spirit of a person so as to ascertain what was the cause of their problem, illness or discomfort. They used the natural forces of nature and the cosmos in ritual or ceremony for divination, along with sacred plants and animals and it was revered as mystical and magical.

Shamans understood that there were natural cosmic forces and laws that governed people's lives and so were able to distinguish from inner pain and external influences much like our healers of today. They understood that a soul lived many lifetimes and had many aspects to it that could be lost or abused, and so did soul retrieval and past life and karmic healings with the use of spirit guides to aid and protect them. They were called upon to help people transcend or cross over into the next world upon dying. Using techniques such as drumming and breath work they rode the waves of consciousness, which could create altered states for themselves and their patients. They knew that to go beyond the rational mind was necessary, for it allowed any inner work on the other planes to be done. This is much like our use of the pranic activation breathing techniques used in a similar manner today.

To become a shaman was an interesting quandary; as with most traditions it seemed to be passed down from within a family in some form, unless they were initiated by spirit in some way and then there was said to be a calling to do this. It was always a learned trade that one took very seriously as one began to understand the supernatural and metaphysical worlds. The decline of shamans throughout the world gave rise to new forms of metaphysical healing en masse, one of these we call reiki. While shamanic practices were and still are considered time-honoured ways of going about all manner of spiritual healing, Reiki is known as another.

I realised that reiki could be considered a form of modern day shamanism, or what would have been called shamanism in other cultures. As I developed my reiki healing practice some spontaneous things began to happen. Some of these took form as inner promptings or spiritual visions during intuitive healings, which helped me to know instinctively what to do. I became aware that the energy of reiki helped awaken the spiritual healer aspects of myself, which is true of many reiki practitioners. Often the dynamics of a reiki healing required that I go beyond my own limitations and perceptions and demanded that I be led, if you like, to places and inner spaces that were very unfamiliar and sometimes very uncomfortable to me. It taught me, in essence, that I had to be flexible and put my total trust into the divine so as to aid in whatever capacity was necessary for the client's highest good, knowing that I was in fact in the arms of God, working God's will for his or her highest good during a healing.

This part of the spiritual healer's teachings seemed to be left out of any manual I had ever read but does, in fact, seem to take place for many a good healer or shaman. These and other things instigated a search for information about traditional shamanism, so I began to read articles and books on the matter. I don't consider myself a shaman or an expert on the subject, however, what I was to discover was very interesting for me as a reiki master and spiritual healer. Reiki and the similarities it has with some aspects of shamanism simply can't be ignored. It is well known that as soon as a reiki practitioner places their hands on a client they go into a light meditative alpha state or trance during healing. Even our modern day hypnotherapy is similar and uses the trance states for the purpose of accessing the subconscious parts of our psyche for re-programming or healing and releasing processes. Reiki, like shamanism, is conducted through altered states of consciousness, which allow well-being and wholeness of energy and spirit to return to a balanced state. These altered states create deep relaxation during reiki which enables the higher self of the patient to do what is needed to bring about balance to its troubled soul, using the healer as a conduit for the spiritual energy required.

During a reiki healing we encounter the vastness of our client's soul and as a result we too have to be prepared to deal with whatever we encounter. Many reiki practitioners, as they progress in their healing ministry, develop and become quite proficient clairvoyants and clairaudients, working with spirit guides as part of their healing, much like shamanism. Those who work on these planes like shamans, often do part soul retrievals and past life healings as are required by the receiver. I have carried out many past life healings and soul rescues during reiki sessions, however, I didn't use ceremony or ritual so much as prayer and intention and the energy of reiki as my focus. Many of us, like shamans, use tools like crystal wands, essences, colour and visionary techniques, usually under guidance and in a conscious altered state (channelling).

Reiki is a process within itself and relies less on the practitioner's ability to heal; rather it accepts that divine will is in fact present with the channelled life force energy and balance occurs, as the person receiving requires it. The practitioner does not usually determine this unless they have developed their spiritual connections or advanced psychic abilities and or commune with guidance from the spirit world. Understanding the soul aspects of the human being is a bit like studying the wind; forever elusive, changing and evolving but nonetheless interesting.

We have now the urban shamans appearing amongst most cultures and their techniques include reiki, herb and flower essences, naturopathy and aromatherapy, hypnotherapy and psychotherapy and the list goes on. Shamanism lives on and is becoming widely accepted in its more modern forms. I believe Dr. Usui did the world a favour when he rediscovered reiki and forged it into the system it is today. As a shamanistic pathway, forging some of our healers of the future, it is second to none. I feel he took ancient shamanic healing wisdom and mixed it with spiritual essence and energy and came up with an amazing healing energy that transcends most things metaphysical that are felt in the physical.

As a transformational path, helping us to relinquish the past and the lower body's egotistical needs, reiki is truly amazing. Unlike shamanism though, reiki is not just for the healers or clairvoyants, it is also for anyone who has the desire to heal themselves and take control of themselves energetically on all levels. As humans we have had many limitations in our experiences of healing ourselves, however, if I have learnt something from reiki it would be that radical unconditional love is the key to real healing on all planes within, and I'm sure most shamans would agree.

21 DAY REIKI SELF CLEANSE

After undergoing the attunement process you will go through some changes, the 21 day self cleanse helps with the integration of the new energy you have received and enables you to begin to feel the energy flow for yourself better.

1. Collect 21 flat stones (or use crystals) number them 1 – 21 with a marker pen or tape.
2. Prepare a list of things you wish to begin to heal, such as attitudes or relationship issues. I suggest you address any remembered life traumas first.
3. As you begin each day of your 21 days of self-treatment you delicate the stone for that day to one from your list of self-healing. You may say let this Reiki treatment heal my "attitude or relationship with "......................" and say the attitude or relationship for that day. Then proceed with your self treatment.
4. Turn the stone over marking the passing of that day. This creates a ritual deepening the meaning of your 21 days of self-treatments. Some people use these stones over & over taking themselves through a regular cleanse as a part of their spiritual journey through Reiki, tuning themselves up as self maintenance. It's especially good for use after each level, using the new reiki symbols given in your attunements. Remember you cannot overdose on this energy for it is self regulating.

The 21 day cleanse idea was shown to me by a New Zealand Reiki Master who has since passed away. Much beloved and blessings to you Maureen Kelly.

Some ideas for use on your 21 day Reiki cleanse.
Take time to think about what you need to focus on.

Day 1 misconceptions, forgiveness or humility
Day 2 relationship with heaven, god, goddess
Day 3 arrogance, anger or rage
Day 4 lack of confidence or needing self-love
Day 5 fears related to any control issues
Day 6 relationship with the famous
Day 7 relationship with money or success
Day 8 marriage / partner, or any personal relationship
Day 9 self connection, soul awareness
Day 10 using all six senses
Day 11 relationship with children
Day 12 issues related with touch or contact
Day 13 unbalanced emotional feelings
Day 14 relationship with friends or parents
Day 15 ability to receive love & personal desires
Day 16 health related issue
Day 17 career, work or purpose
Day 18 areas you feel blocked or stagnant
Day 19 anxiety, or not feeling safe
Day 20 relationship with self
Day 21 grief, death and dying

Some Recommended Reading to aid your Cosmic Reiki journey:

The Force, by Stuart Wild
Earth Angels, by Doreen Virtue
Real Magic, by Wayne Dwyer
Essential Reiki, by Diane Stein
Hands of Light, by Barbara Anne Brennan
Light Emerging, by Barbara Anne Brennan
How to Heal Your Life, by Lousie Hay
Hawaya Takata's Story, by Helen Haberly
The Celestine Prophecy, by James Redfield
Whispering Winds of Change, by Stuart Wilde
Reiki Universal Life Energy, by B. Baginski & S. Sharamon
The Body is the Barometer of the Soul, by Annette Noontil
Miracles by Stuart Wilde
God I Am by Peter O Erbe
Living with Joy by Sanaya Roman
The Power of NOW by Eckhart Tolle
Love is Letting go of Fear by Ken Keyes
Radical Forgiveness by Colin C. Tipping
Return to Love by Marianne Williamson
One Step Forward for Reiki by A. J. Mackenzie
Ageless Body Timeless Mind by Deepak Chopra
The Challenge to Teach Reiki by A. J. Mackenzie Clay
The Complete Reiki Handbook by Lotus Light - Shangri La
Awakening to the Tao by Liu I-Ming translated by Thomas Cleary
Men are from Mars Woman are from Venus by John Gray
Opening to Channel by Sanaya Roman and Duane Packer
Reiki- Way of the Heart by Lotus Light - Shangri La
The Prophet and other books by Kahlil Gibran
Miles Beyond Reiki by A. J. Mackenzie Clay
The Chakras by C. W. Leadbeater
Going Within by Shirely MacLean

OTHER BOOKS & ORACLES
by the author S'Roya Rose

S'Roya Rose TAROT
78 Card Deck and Guidebook

Modern Goddess Oracle
60 Cards & Guidebook

The Art of Meaningful Living
Simple Wisdom for the 21st Century

Blue Moon Oracle
52 Oracle Cards & Guidebook

S'ROYA ROSE
www.sroyarose.com
email@sroyarose.com

3RD EYE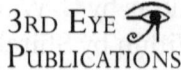
PUBLICATIONS

Embracing the Power
of the Goddess

TAROT A Sacred Doorway
A must have Tarot Compendium
for the Modern Cosmic Sage!

In Search of SOUL
Who am I? Why am I here? What's my
Purpose?

CHAKRAS
& Their Hidden Wisdom

The Third EYE
Psychic Secrets for aspiring Mystics

For more information on,
or to stock or purchase any of
S'Roya's book titles or oracle
card decks or magazines,
please visit her website:
www.sroyarose.com
or alternatively
www.phoenixdistribution.com.au

ABOUT S'ROYA

S'Roya is a gifted clairvoyant Psycho Therapist, and well known Australian Celebrity Psychic Medium, she is an initiating High Priestess of the Goddess, who works with the angelic, elemental, Ascended Masters, ancient Mystics, the Animal clans, and other cosmic Shamanic realms, able to connect with spirit guides and deceased loved ones.

Having appeared nationally on channel Seven's 'New Age of Aquarius' show, and on channel nine's 'Sunday Show', she also makes guest appearances on Psychic TV OZ. She has been teaching Reiki and the Tarot, facilitating Spiritual and Psychic development workshops and running Goddess and psychic circles for 18 years.

An accomplished writer, she's has been active in shifting consciousness publishing various book titles having been the creatrix and editor of many spiritual magazines ie; Deja Vu, Dharma, BlackRose, Goddess Guru & Avalon. Recently she launched her amazing Modern Goddess Oracle deck and her latest fabulous Blue Moon Oracle wisdom cards.

A natural born Mystic of the modern age she is respected as being a wise goddess, her counsel being constantly sought after, usually bookings must be made weeks in advance. To find out more about her Reiki Seminars or book a personal session, or have a Reading with S'Roya or a Healing Psycho Therapy session, simply email her on:

email@sroyarose.com ~ www.sroyarose.com

www.ingramcontent.com/pod-product-compliance
Lightning Source LLC
Chambersburg PA
CBHW071424160426
43195CB00013B/1801